DIS... RD

go

"I just read your new manuscript and got the same feeling I had some weeks ago when I was back in Chicago in a cab very early in the morning on my way to catch a train, the city shrouded in a misty rain, and as we passed what has always been one of my favorite historic intersections by the river at michigan and wacker (where once long long ago the freshly created soul of jazz poured out of the London House) there was this fucking sign, TRUMP, like an obscenity scrawled across chicago history, illuminated like a raw scar. There's that sense to your book, the scars of how the city was made are part of the architecture, of the landscape."

—Stuart Dybek, author of *The Coast of Chicago*, recipient of a MacArthur Foundation Fellowship

"The stories and personalities memorialized in these poems are real to me. Poet Kevin Coval breathes them back alive with word-pictures both concrete and passionate, compressing centuries into verse. These are poems to be savored. I'd be hard-pressed to pick just one favorite from this remarkable collection."

—Timuel D. Black, Chicago historian/activist/teacher, author of *Bridges of Memory: Chicago's First Wave of Black Migration*

"Kevin Coval has given us a gift, a collection of heartfelt, piercing poems, stories really, about America's city. Taken together, these song-like postcards are a kind of celebration, as well as some takedowns, of those who sweat and struggle and endure to make this city a better place. The book soars."

—Alex Kotlowitz, author of *There Are No Children Here* and *Never a City So Real*

"From our first resident, Jean Baptiste Point du Sable, to the immigrants, migrants, and souls who make this city great, a vibrant, dynamic collection of vignettes that expose the naked truth of our fair city."

—Karen Lewis, teacher and president of the Chicago Teachers Union, Local 1

"Kevin Coval is a dazzling, dizzying time traveler and cultural historian-poet. He is a lover of language, rhythms, and colors and the people who transform in these. He knows the stories of Chicago and all its people—Red, Black, White, Brown, Asian, Queer, Straight. The spine of this book is the people's resistance and struggle for justice and a fair shake. But—not to worry—Kevin puts it all to you so sweetly, so energetically, so for real—he makes you smile behind poem after poem. And then again he makes you want to rise up. He's in the Chicago tradition—fire, earth, and endless blues."

—Angela Jackson, author of *Where I Must Go*, winner of the American Book Award

"An epic that is both intimate and sweeping... Coval's poems not only bridge the past and the present; they create a community through history, returning the city to those who built and continue to build it."

—Lovia Gyarkye, *New Republic*

A
PEOPLE'S
HISTORY
OF
CHICAGO

✱ ✱ ✱ ✱

Kevin Coval

Chicago, Illinois
Haymarket Books

Published in 2017 by
Haymarket Books
P.O. Box 180165
Chicago, IL 60618
773-583-7884
www.haymarketbooks.org
info@haymarketbooks.org

ISBN: 978-1-60846-671-9

Trade distribution:
In the US, Consortium Book Sales and Distribution, www.cbsd.com
In Canada, Publishers Group Canada, www.pgcbooks.ca
In the UK, Turnaround Publisher Services, www.turnaround-uk.com
All other countries, Publishers Group Worldwide, www.pgw.com

This book was published with the generous support of Lannan Foundation and
     Wallace Action Fund.

Cover design by Brett Nieman. Cover photograph by Bob Simpson of a July
2016 sit-in and march against police violence initiated by four teenage women,
which was punctuated by periods of silence and performances of poetry.

Printed in Canada by union labor.

Library of Congress Cataloging-in-Publication data is available.

10 9 8 7 6 5 4 3 2

If history is to be creative, to anticipate a possible future without denying the past, it should, I believe, emphasize new possibilities by disclosing those hidden episodes of the past when, even if in brief flashes, people showed their ability to resist, to join together, occasionally to win.
—Howard Zinn, *A People's History of the United States*

Contents

Foreword

We got the cheat codes.

There's no other place on earth where you can go to a centralized space and see thirteen-, fourteen-, fifteen-, sixteen-, seventeen-, and eighteen-year-olds who want to conquer art and music. I left Chicago for a little and went to LA. But have you ever seen a raw-ass tree or a raw-ass plant that's beautiful, that's fully bloomed and growing? It can't fully bloom if you uproot it. If you take it somewhere else, out of its natural environment, it's not gonna grow the same way. If you take a tree out of the dirt, a Christmas tree, and move it into your crib, it'll stay that exact same tree for a little while before it starts to wilt, but it won't grow anymore. You can't uproot a plant. You have to let it grow. If I were to have grown in LA, I might've grown into some shit I'm not supposed to be or just not grown at all, or just peaked. I can reach my peak in Chicago cuz that's where I was planted and where I can continue to grow.

I had planned on living in LA, but when I was out there going to parties and feeling that vibe, I thought it was ungodly, it wasn't true to who I was born to be or what I was supposed to grow to be. Being there made me realize this is not where I'm supposed to get my biggest experiences. As sad as I ever was in LA, the lowest I've ever been, it's not where my lowest was supposed to be. The highest I've been, the happiest I've been in Los Angeles, was not where my life's happiest moments were supposed to be. Being happy means doing what you are supposed to do, being exactly who you are supposed to be. My god, my inner understanding, whatever it is that guides me, had me recognizing that I'm not supposed to be there.

We have a head start. If you've been in that building once, in the Harold Washington Library, one time, you know. Harold Washington. The first Black mayor of Chicago. A very powerful man. A very connected man. A very humble and grounded man. A household name who died in office while at work. His library is in the center of downtown, in the center of the Loop, where all the trains meet. For us to walk into that building is astounding. My dad volunteered for Harold Washington. That's how he got his record expunged. That's how he dodged the system. Years later, he has a library named after him and I could walk in from the cold and experience this temple.

From the age of fourteen, I was trying to go against the grain, to grow into a time and period where it's dope to be anti-establishment, where it's dope to not just accept all the answers that are given to you but to look for your own answers. I am trying to push that. I'm trying to push that to other people who didn't get taught that. As kids that grew up in the '90s and early 2000s, we are able to ask questions like *What's going on? Who are the people leading us? Who are those people teaching us? What are they telling us? How are they able to tell us that? Who are they and where are they coming from and is it the truth?* I've been taught to be a critical thinker, and I was able to say this doesn't feel right. Having the understanding I've been blessed with, I've been able to discern that that shit is not right, that it doesn't feel right, that it doesn't seem right.

I met Kevin Coval at an orientation at Jones College Prep, the first time I ever went into my high school cuz I didn't check it out beforehand. I just signed up for it and applied. So my first time going up to the school was for the Louder Than A Bomb team orientation and Kevin was doing a writing workshop. Though I didn't make my slam team or to Louder Than A Bomb, Kevin ended up being very instrumental to me.

Kevin Coval is my artistic father. He mentored my friends Malcolm London and Dimress Dunnigan and Fatimah Warner and got me shows, and those shows got me a little bit of bread and the confidence to continue and take the craft seriously. In a lot of ways he was the other side of Brother Mike for me, and anybody from Chicago knows what that means and how big a statement that is. He was that for me and for a lot of people.

Kevin made art a job to me. He made me feel like it was real. He made me feel like the competition was real. He made me feel that the money was real. He made me feel that the love and the fans were real. And if I didn't have him in my life I would've been complacent. He took me out of that space and made me understand what it is to be a poet, what it is to be an artist, and what it is to serve the people.

Chance the Rapper
Chance the Chicagoan

Shikaakwa

before 1492

sea of tall grass. sky quiet
enough to hear yourself think.
ancestors talk shit where the wind
whips brisk from the lake. the face
of the river ripples. land of marsh.
before the steel plow
& forced removal

    this was *shikaakwa*:

wild leek, onion, garlic. a great
trade center, hundreds of tribes
canoed to the portage to barter fish
& skins, squash & bone, mix languages
& blood: home of Chippewa, Potawatomi
Kickapoo, Ho-Chunk, Ottawa, Miami, Ioway
Sauk, Fox, Blackhawk, Odawa & Illinois.

thousands of years before joliet, lasalle
daley, podmajersky, before tribes were razed,
lakes polluted, the blood diseased, the people
rounded into prisons, reservations, Maywood.

there were ash trees, elms & basswood, oak
hickory. history was stories your elders sang.
the young danced rain & memory awake.
there were thousands, before. this land, a sacred
burial ground, a people we delete.

        quiet

before your morning paper
put your ear to the earth
hear the terror of the horses
the wails of the hunters
howling in this city of wind
on this land of skunk, the stench
of blood inescapable.

lasalle Wrote It Down Wrong
1687

gringoed the whole place.
every street & building some flat
mispronunciation, some misshapen
mouth   some murder.

Chicagua wild
garlic in indigenous
utterance.   some funk
music.   some rampant weed
returning, perennial & persistent.

Chicago is malignant, a mass
of machinery built upon mass graves.
the beginning of a long death march.
an inadequate water
down. an erasure, an eraser
pink as the whiteman's tongue.

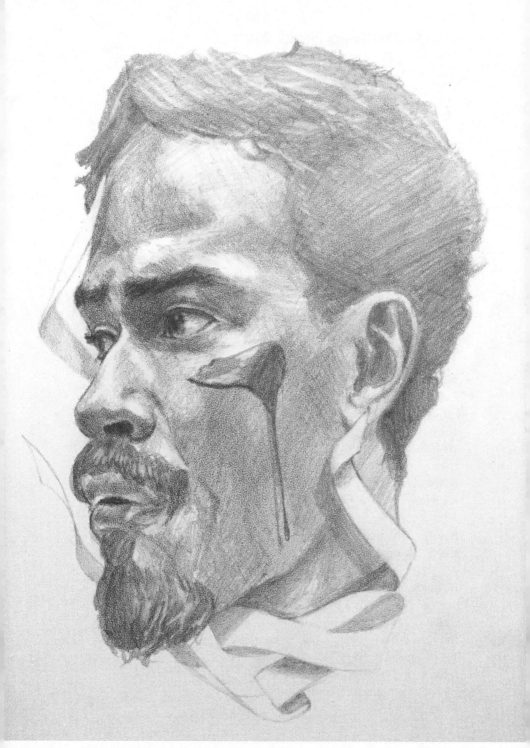

The Father Is a Black Man
1779

> *There is not a single street in the city of Chicago named in honor of the Black man*
> *who founded this city, not an alley...but John Kinzie, a white man, who came after*
> *DuSable, when DuSable was forced out or pushed out or whatever, he ended up*
> *with DuSable's property, and Kinzie has a bridge, Kinzie has a street, Kinzie has a*
> *building, and all he did was buy DuSable's house.*
> **Lerone Bennett, Jr.**

the father is mixed. the father is Black.
his mother a slave. his father a french
mariner. the first non-Native
to settle in Chicago
Jean Baptiste Point duSable
was a hustler.
he worked the trap.
traded pelts at the frontier.
married Kittihawa
a Potawatomi woman
he saw sailing the Mississippi.
the traditional ceremony
officiated by a Chief.
the father was cool
with the Indigenous.
they settled at the mouth
of the river, where the tribune sits
spewing untruths in english.
DuSable spoke spanish, french, english
& several Native dialects.
the father a genius.

he made okra & oxtails
with sos pwa noir, a black bean
sauce, & joumou, a pumpkin stew
harvested from the acres he farmed.
his house had a large stone fireplace
a piano, a garden & orchard.
he collected paintings, mirrors
& walnut furniture.

the father had style
and maybe some gators.
he finessed pesos, pounds & francs
from folks traveling thru town, down
the river, out west or back east. he stayed
serving. awash in wampums. the father was ballin.

his granddaughter, the first non-Native born
in Chicago, was mixed. the first child was mixed.

the father, a product
of terror & rape.
the father, the city
forgets, is mixed

the mix made the British
nervous. a body protestants
couldn't wrap their heads around.

the father is a Black man
pushed out by a white man
rich & thirsty.

DuSable left to die
far from the city
built with his hands.

his mixed hands.
his Black hands.

the father is a Black man.

The Treaty of Chicago
September 26, 1833[1]

> *Our land has been wasting away ever since the white people became our neighbors,*
> *and we have now hardly enough left to cover the bones of our tribe.*
> **(Potawatomi) Chief Metea**

getting the Chiefs to sign
wouldn't be easy. in 1795
the Greenville treaty stole
six miles around the mouth
of the River. city of long cons
fire & fine print. the fight
at Fort Dearborn whites wouldn't
forget, when the Miami tribe
embarrassed the fumbling army
of dumb settlers in fifteen minutes
to take back Roosevelt & Michigan
land simply called earth then.
                 but this'll be the last time
the indigenous dance at the waterway
connecting the Mississippi to the Great Lakes,
a trade post between the Caribbean & New York.
the perfect nexus for whiskey & unbridled capitalism.
this town, such desirable waterfront property
the government will kill to own it.

the pioneers plied Chiefs
all night with bourbon. under intoxication
duress & gun powder, under disease
& white power, in english, an illiterate theft.
they marked the parchment, *X*

Hog Butcher for the World
December 25, 1865[2]

grid of flesh. source
of labor & meal & mayhem.
cutting edge ingenuity to maim
& murder. a grand dis-assembly
line. innovator of the killing wheel.
steak knife. craver of cattle
earth. neighborhoods gutted. chest
opened by a butcher
                              block
by block.   dissected
like 7th grade science / class.

Chicago is a frog.
Chicago is a pig   fetus

splayed & separated
                                    segregated
from its body
                         politic.
white meat   dark.
an experiment the country watches
                                       & repeats.

town of   viaducts
blvd   motes.
turf wars   & stop signs.
one ways   & circuitous routes.
folks   & people.
          a park
                in between.
                a metra train.

          eminent domain.

          the body
quartered.   broken
                              down

                                        somewhere.
                                                    picked over
a blueprint
refined.   a carcass
                        city
                            of scraps
                                & sausage.

Albert Parsons Can Hang
November 11, 1887

Lay bare the inequities of capitalism; expose the slavery of law; proclaim the tyranny of government; denounce the greed, cruelty, abominations of the privileged class.
Albert Parsons[3]

a dumb kid of privilege.
a son of the south.
a descendant of the american revolution.
as a boy, he fought with the confederates.
as a man, he apologized to the Black woman who raised him.
a lover of Lucy,
       part Mestizo & Black radical socialist,
       more dangerous than a thousand rioters.
a typesetter like my grandfather.
a believer in the rights of the worker.
an 8-hour day & 8 to sleep & 8 to play.
a ringer of the alarm.
a white tiger, before Huey, maybe
       dynamite, Jimmie Walker
an organizer in the good times
       summer sunday beer gardens.
a longing for bread or blood.
a leader in the rise of the working class.
a target the barons went after.
an albatross to the merchant prince marshall field.
a defendant in the Haymarket Riot
       no evidence, no fair jury
       railroaded by george pullman.
Albert Parsons
a white man to become
a white man who acted
a white man unbound
       by guilt or other bullshit
a prisoner in cell 29
a writer, live from death row.

How to Be Down
September 18, 1889

Jane Addams from rural Cedarville.
originated in loot & leisure. got shook
the world wasn't like that for all
so she built a table, a house, not perfect
but bout it bout it. her living room big
enough for the whole West Side. kneading
culture as bread & spaghetti eventually
& kindergarten too & garbage pickup
& public parks, a place for immigrants
& a place for Benny Goodman to swing
& Upton Sinclair to report, & W. E. B. Du Bois
to prophesy. a place for Ida B. Wells to debate
& educate Ellen Gates Starr, Florence Kelley
Alice Hamilton, this squad of white women
led by a squat Queer woman. how odd indeed.
how down
                    she be.

The L Gets Open
June 6, 1892

the loop would be next.
for now a line, a track
one neighborhood   to another.
magic. transit. a new   street
      different block.   the ethnic lock
          picked
by a steam engine   a camel
          thru the eye
of a needle.
viaduct   crosser. 39th Street
                   to Congress
     31 blocks.
            a working
class
   spaceship   to fly
above
   ground
     & borders.

     all   city
   ours.

The white City
May 1, 1893

the world's fair turned the swamp
utopian lie. classical architecture
a garish nod to old ass empire,
made the poet of steel, Louis Sullivan,
mourn the buildings businessmen
desired to show off. all bluster
& facade. all fronts. the white city
meant to distract, erase the Black
city of smoke & sky, grime & grind.
faces that gutted the land, made it run,
banned, pushed to the side. the face
the city presented to tourists, miles
of magnificence millionaires wanted
out-of-towners to whisper about
on the train trip home. a museum
prison Houdini tried escaping.
fraudulent city of the future built
from scratch, from scraps, hidden
the hands that scraped. beneath
the veneer lurked murder. silent
terror behind white construction.

Eugene Debs Reads Marx in Prison
1895

like Malcolm, memorized the dictionary.

*Nature does not produce*⁴ subjugated
steps. every eve he'd walk the yard
breathing beneath *night's curtain.*
the free sky etched into his head. *on the one side*
owners of money or commodities, on the other men
possessing nothing but their own labour-power
contemplating ways to counter empire.
in *midnight's throne, this relation has no natural basis.*
like the imagination, the heavens spread
common to all historical periods, pages lit
by moon turn. liberated from these walls
he'll walk, waving a new, red banner.

Reversing the Flow of the Chicago River

January 2, 1900

there's shit in the water.
to avoid typhoid fever
an engineering miracle
on par with the pyramids.
canal & quarry men lost
their lives & didn't get credit
or fair compensation. before
it's over Governor Altgeld calls
the national guard to kill some on strike.

                                    but today

Chicago does the impossible.
reverses the flow away
from the great lake michigan
toward the des plaines river
& lockport: this very moment
a man-made nile, a diversion
of millions   of gallons.
by crane & crook
neck, backs breaking rock.
millennia of earth blown with dynamite.
the grit of workers carved a path, bent
the south branch & main stem.
dug 28 miles of canal in the long
purple dusk of a new century.
the sweat & calloused hands
of 8,500 men did the impossible:
shifted the norm
for the health of the young
metropolis. immigrant men
a force, to counter the natural system
so the city   could survive.

The Great Migration
1915–1950

No longer do our lives depend upon the soil, the sun, the rain or the wind; we live by the grace of jobs and the brutal logic of jobs.
Richard Wright, *12 Million Black Voices*

The Defender said come: here
is a promised   land. fill the factories.
the train travels north. leaves at dusk.
leaves the Delta. the train forward
lurches where earth hardens into sky
rises into steel. still Black in the 8 hours
(at least) of chaos. here accents foreign
fast. *a*'s stretch like restrictive covenants
circling Bronzeville. the city builds heaven
for a few. tenements for most. a project
to carve a moment of quiet in the roar
& rumble of machine. lines more rigid
by the minute. lines visible & not;
at the beach, on the train, schools
banks. lines shift, sharpen, root thick.
blueprint into bars: which ones to go
into & not. neighborhoods demarcated
sounds nothing like democracy. separate
& nothing equal. sections. housing
authorities. prisons, windows open
air, industrial, capital, labor under
a different overseer, a different punch
clock. in, off hours, invent in the domestic
space with wares brought from the south
the other side of the atlantic, made electric,
sped up & swinging, Jack Johnson. A. Philip
Randolph will rise from this earth;
a Black mayor, a Black president.

everything will change & nothing will

The Eastland Disaster

July 24, 1915

*Grim industrial feudalism stands with dripping and red hands behind the whole
Eastland affair.*
> **Carl Sandburg**

saturday morning, at 6:30 am
western electric workers were ordered
to be on time & dress their best
at the wharf. too poor for holiday
they scrambled in excitement: packed
day bags & made sure dirt disappeared
from their children's faces & fingernails.

the company men would travel to Michigan City
by carriage & the mighty Eastland would carry
secretaries, bean counters, ledger keepers & factory
workers across the great blue body of lake.

the boat'd had problems before.
no one seemed to care. it was
top-heavy like the economy,
the hubris of the city's
over-fed owners.

an hour in, the ship shifted
twenty feet from the shore.
in the middle of the Chicago
river, the boat turned, a whale
of metal flipping on its belly.
hundreds fell from the open
upper deck like drunken pigeons.
hundreds trapped in rooms
beneath, crushed by dead pianos
& falling furniture. mouths stuffed
with gallons of roaring river water

844 people, mostly immigrants
mostly workers died in the Eastland.
my great-grandmother among them.

after my grandfather turned
bastard & stalked the north side
with a two-by-four on his shoulder
like the city owed him something
& it did.

The Murder of Eugene Williams

July 27, 1919

the summer was hot as hell.

for relief, his boys brought a raft
to the beach at 25th Street the whole
city's body laid out on water.

lake michigan's powerful current
dragged the raft a few blocks south
a/cross an invisible line in the water.
at 29th Street rocks flew. launched
from white hands on land
they thought theirs alone, to own.
one rocked the temple of Eugene, 17,
off the raft. he drowned in the body
at the bottom of the lake.

& again water graves claim Black
& again white police refuse to arrest
& again white gangs rally

from bridgeport, back of the yards.
white gangs like the hamburgs
like richie daley's crew, like the future
mayors

.

Society for Human Rights
(America's First Gay Rights Organization)
December 10, 1924

at 17, the boy's admitted
into an insane asylum.
institution of electroshock
& hallucinogens, white coats
& sodomy laws. the state
not separated from the church.
they wanted the devil out. he became
double-O seven. shaken & stirred
to action.

Henry Gerber wasn't his name.
a german immigrant boy hiding
in america's skirt. told to meld into
the heteronorm. the boy made illegal.
his fatherland wrote paragraph 175[5]
the bible an arm against him. an outlaw.
an outcast   would go crazy.
        he called a community
together. organized a society
in secret. a space for men to gather
in his home in old town, untouched
by the fear of being found out
& detained & shamed.

John Graves, a Black minister
whose partner was a Pullman porter,
his friend, comrade & confidant signed
the papers to become the first
president of the first organization
in the dumb country, in the young city
45 years before stonewall. Black & White
Chicago men mustered a congregation
                            until they couldn't
until Henry Gerber was fired from his post
office job, arrested, tried three times & lost
his life savings.

he'd go underground, go pseudonym
write newsletter Connection chronicles
from lone apartment bunkers, advocating
for the safety of his being & the being
of those like him & the country being ok
with his being & those like him & the city
country being greater because of it.

Thomas Dorsey, Gospel's Daddy
1932

before the unspeakable
he was Georgia Tom on the road
with Ma Rainey, a raunchy hit maker

seven million records sold.
then his wife Nettie died
in labor. his son two days later.

grief is an unshakeable shelter.
like Coltrane composing *Love
Supreme* in his child's afterglow

Dorsey took to song to mourn
channeled the spirit of rhythm
& blues in juke & segregated joints.

he harnessed the secular
for the sanctified. *Take My Hand,
Precious Lord* the genesis. gospel

called Dorsey's. praise
with piano & tambourine, returning
Black Jesus to the choir, to the ladies

of the church to raise & transform
him, white & stiff on the cross
as he was, into a movement Dr. King

messed with. no one wanted to
publish the songs he sang. so
he made his own label: House

of Music; independent, divine. self
-determined. tryin to run the devil
out; white, blue-eyed or otherwise.

Gwendolyn Brooks Stands in the Mecca

1936

I wrote about what I saw and heard in the street. There was my material.
Gwendolyn Brooks

she slang snake oils
at 19. her small hands
moving love potions
out bottles for some kind
of doctor. stalking halls
listening to the masses
stuffed in kitchenettes.
blocks of brick. floors
of Black lives. every
day people fighting
& fucking & struggling
to make it. sometimes
they didn't. nose ripe
with onion fumes
rising like the people's
will in the warpland.
she took rich snapshots
of the poor. some rhythm
rattling around her head.
each sound an ornament:
a key turning the tumbler,
faucets praising the body
with lukewarm water,
the laughter of kids
& criminals. the lost
girls. she kept count
of them, each syllable
stuck in a handbag
in her head, waiting
til she got home
to lay every precious
note on the table
right in front of her
nose, the tiny gems
she'd gather thru

the day, all
the ingredients
she'd need to sit
& begin to write
a new literature,
a new world.

Hansberry vs. Lee

November 12, 1940

american racism helped kill him
Lorraine Hansberry

her father knew a good deal
when he saw it. a real estate
man building a Black belt
in Bronzeville growing
like a belly spilling into Woodlawn.
the whites got to clutching their pearls.
built picket fences taller, whiter. guarded
them with ordinances nobody voted for
& bombs that burst in Black homes freely
as the 4th of July.
                Carl stayed strapped
with lawyers, reading endless court documents
in the wee hours under dimming light
& the coming dawn. Du Bois & Robeson
ate in the kitchen when they were in town
encouraging him to fight & bust the barriers down
all the way up   to the supreme court
                          he went.

& little Lorraine,
ten years old at betsy ross
elementary, listened in the corner
with Langston in her lap,
taking notes the whole
time, writing down her father's face
how it sagged, sad, what he said.
his wrestling & anguish. her diary
became the first Black woman
on broadway, the great white way.
the story of her daddy's fight, how even
victory is death for Black men
in america.

Muddy Waters Goes Electric

1945

bars & rent parties roar. motherfuckers won't shut up.
the acoustic guitar's an impotent whimper in the throat
of war machines. some country shit won't cut it.
Muddy slick, like his hair, like the puddles & creeks
he played in, in Clarksdale.   a long way

from sharecropping & his dead mama.
he drives a truck delivering venetian blinds & works
a paper mill making lumber lay like linen.

Uncle Joe got him an ax with fangs. he plugged in
& shook fire out. the amp spit licks that wrapped
around necks of macks talkin weak game & zip.
fuck a pick, it remind him too much of Mississippi.
pluck this metal with hands that worked the earth,
that call folk home & throw them thru the future
out a plate glass window. he a conjured a time
machine.
                    (white boys tried to it pick up
but couldn't access its Black magic. clapton,
a poor mimic. the stones, a colonial bore.)

McKinley Morganfield sits up on a stool
around 43rd Street & shoots lightning out
his fingers, a jolt thru the city. he makes
the blues jump. he shocks the world.

Nelson Algren Meets Simone de Beauvoir at the Palmer House

February 21, 1947

beneath ornate ceilings, in the grand room
on plush cushions, they drank martinis
he couldn't stomach & she didn't understand
a word he said. he thought she looked
like a french school teacher, a good-lookin one
who in a few days he'd read about in
the new yorker. he's a different sort, she thought.
not like the men she'd tolerate in the parisian cafe society,
high-minded intellectuals who'd rather talk than lust.

she returned in april. he took her
to the polish bars in wicker park,
to his apartment without a bathroom,
garbage piling in the alleys. he'd show
her a jail, the electric chair, men strung
on heroin. a city/country taking it
on the chin. he had a chip
on his shoulder, a second city complex.

she's a modern wave french Feminist.
the loved, lauded, chic Queen of the existentialists.

he's a Chicago artist cursed in the middle, unappreciated
in a moment McCarthy will try to ban his realism & wit.

she loved his grit, the precision of craft
honed thru years of devotion. the gift
of pen & more. he made her come
to his city again & for the first time.

they were destined
to nose dive. be out
of reach. an impossible
bird & bear bound
to the cities that made them.

Algren died without anyone
claiming his body. his heart
attacking minutes after
a reporter asked of her.

de Beauvoir was buried
alongside Sartre in Paris
but bore Algren's silver
ring on her bone, forever.

Pickle with a Peppermint Stick
white flight after World War II, 1948–1978

Integration is the period between the arrival of the first Black and the departure of the last white.
Saul Alinsky

                              is some
                         Maxwell Street hold over.
                        brine, tangy. crisp since 1898
                     when the first wave of immigrant
                     jews slid safe from europe & made
                 shtetls. schmattas tied over the wide
                 hips of Bubbes preparing vegetables
                 for the hawk & long winter ahead. a
                 pickle's perfect for lunch, some snack
                 out a jar: garlic, peppercorn & dill.
                 enterprise young hustler. henry ford
                 off the block. out the hood. innovate.
                 dream america in the trunk & church
                 of the dollar. amass. mass produce in
                 plastic. produce plastic. exit the shtetl
             for the shrubs of the suburbs. leave relics
             in the corner store. leave poor, darker new
         immigrants behind in the corner store. leave
     something for them to suck on. the South Side
         became the new north, became the old south.
             Harriet's railroad stopped too soon. shtetls
         grew ghettos. Blacks from the south, stopped
         on the stoop, but the stoop already claimed.
         the corner already owned by someone else.
         Jim Crow lives here too. the sour too much
         to take after coming all that way. the north
         promised roads of gold & bellies of milk.
         salt & vinegar too much bitter to swallow.
             too much history to inherit & repeat.
         the peppermint stick is some sweet/ness
         to help america go down. some castor
         oil & BBQ. some addition & innovation
         kids with hot tongues playing with fire
         demanded for fun, a change of pace &
         palate they shanked the pickle with
         a peppermint stick like a vd exam.
         something here is sick & burning.
             here's some cool to extinguish
                 the fire, some mint to ease
                     all this funk.

Sun Ra Becomes a Synthesizer

October 20, 1952

> *I'm not a minister, I'm not a philosopher, I'm not a politician, I'm in another category.*
> -Sun Ra

thecollegedropoutconscientiousobjector
EgyptologistBlackfuturistGarveyiteoccultist
interplanetarytranshistoricalorator. at night
he played bump & grind in Cal City strip clubs
but in the small apartment in Washington Park
he learned to synthesize: Themi research, race
etymologist fusing ideas & tone in dissonance
& modality. minor, major sound effects to swing
to rocket fly towards an Afro-Future. wheeling
mimeographed dissertations on 55th Street
politicking with Black Muslims & Hebrew Israelites
in a gold Pharaoh nemes headdress & glitter cape.
today he shed his slave name & Herman Blount
became Sun Ra, a vessel taking trips to Saturn
way before any white man made it to the moon.

hugh hefner, a Play Boy

December 1953

A woman reading Playboy *feels a little like a Jew reading a Nazi manual.*
Gloria Steinem

his first wife Mildred cheated. her guilt
assuaged. she allowed him to play, boy.

they split. he boasted of the twelve cover girls
in a subscription cycle, he'd bed eleven. never pay, boy.

captain of industry & sexual harassment, selling
the dream. a new hi-fi. just press play, boy.

the parties, a wink, a club house, cosby friend
offering quaaludes, *thigh openers.* he preyed, boy.

flaccid maleness. plastic surgery, eurocentric
ageless, airbrushed. his fantasy, a play. boy

with a mansion. potato chips & porn. knockoff
chic, convinced he's a bon vivant, a playboy.

skin stretched, ascot knot over his gizzard. silk pajama sleaze.
when he realize G-d's feminine, he'll wish he woulda prayed, boy.

the walt disney of misogyny, mainstreaming objectification. bunnies
splayed bare, just supposed to lay there, silent, in playboy.

Mamie Till Bears the Movement

Roberts Temple Church of G-d, 4021 S. State St.
September 3, 1955

I wanted the world to see what they did to my baby.
Mamie Till-Mobley

Mamie told 'em keep the casket open.
Mamie told 'em keep the casket open.
Mamie told 'em keep the casket open.
Mamie told 'em keep the casket open.
Mamie told 'em keep the casket open.
Mamie told 'em keep the casket open.
Mamie told 'em keep the casket open.
Mamie told 'em keep the casket open.
Mamie told 'em keep the casket open.
Mamie told 'em keep the casket open.
Mamie told 'em keep the casket open.
Mamie told 'em keep the casket open.
Mamie told 'em keep the casket open.
Mamie told 'em keep the casket open.

king daley Unfurls His burnham Plan
1958–1965

daley's plan took
105 acres in one fell swoop.
closed the entry point to immigrants
from everywhere. one of the only
integrated neighborhoods,
old Maxwell Street.

the wives of city workers organized
protests. jammed their aged, round
bodies into his fifth floor city hall office
to throw books & foreign expletives
at the mayor who sighed & turned
a dumb, dead ear & corned-beef heart.

UIC is built in the architectural style of brutalism.
what was said to be a bridge to the community
was a concrete casket. a cement balloon
expanding on inflated budgets & the mayor's hot air
a big bad wolf blowing houses down. eight thousand
people displaced. six hundred businesses.
the campus a typhoon on the near west side.
university hall a grave marker, a castle
in the heavens. the administration looks down
like the peregrine falcons who made refuge
on the 28th floor: birds of a feather, predators of the sky.

The Division Street Riots
June 12, 1966

the summer of the first
Puerto Rican Day parade, the hood
bomba-d in the face of imperialists.
cops felt some type of way. chased
Aracelis Cruz thru alleys & shot him
in the back. neighbors stepped
off porches, from in front of coolers
to assist the young man laying
on the ground in the lot near Damen
& the police protected the land
grab with batons & brute force & beat
abuelitas armed with only chancletas.

for 2 days, Division became the Island
unified. the sun rose & soon the metal
flags. the iron of Oscar Lopez. Humboldt
Park to La Clark, Puerto Ricans aligned
across redlines with Panthers, a coalition
of Brown & Black, the bosses' greatest fear.
Division Street became a gauntlet
a proving ground. Cha Cha Jimenez[6]
would feel the earth quiver & kneel
before its majesty, in isolation, in county
throwing up junk & sins & the Young
Lords will rise like the sun
& daughters & sons will defend
abuelitas armed with chancletas
in the name of the island & ancient
G-ds, in solidarity & self-determination.

the fight, the stand
the stake in the land

from here, a people
will not move.

Martin Luther King Prays in Marquette Park

August 5, 1966

> *That is no Jerusalem on Lake Michigan.*
> **MLK**

he journeyed to the hot
cauldron of the South Side
to pry apartments open. make them
livable, not slumlord roach traps.
his people here told him not to.
Jesse & nem warned these white clans
weren't a dumb collection of farm hands.
the whole city's a white gang.

but King couldn't listen with all the blood in his ear.

in the month the poor & old
wilt cuz the city whites & boils
bricks, sticks & epithets flew.
one rocked King in the crown.
brought him to his knees. made
his blood faucet & mix with dirt
white men stole & misspelled.

what curse did he utter
beneath his breath, onto the land
we reek of & revel in.
what prayer did he plant.
what whisper raised
a forest, a Chairman Fred.

what mark of Cain did he cut
into the park named for french colonists
into the city of no peace. his blood
a potion that parted a sea to lead whites
to the land promised in schaumburg
a sham burg, a death. a dead; see
america in parts. a King bent
beneath the furnace mouth
of a white mass, an american
church, a dragon he couldn't slay.

Studs Terkel Drops a Mixtape
January 16, 1967[7]

it started in the lobby of his parents'
boarding house; a thousand colloquialisms
& idiosyncratic speech patterns. it started
with a kid in a cab, the discipline
of empathy. the tape recorder
a time machine. a teleporter. mirror
& mountaintop. it started talking
to 200 everyday people. no celebrity.
edited 70. ages 15 to 90: bar owners & alcoholics,
a Native American boiler man, activists,
racists, teachers & the forgotten who live
alone in furnished rooms. populism
on the page. guerilla journalism
before it was called that. it started
in Bug House Square: the denizen forum
for radicals & miscreants, the genius & insane
lines blurred, irrelevant. here is the collected
memory of a city that is the country
the microcosm. the division in us all.

Carl Sandburg Village (Where My Parents Met)
1967–1969

When we did Sandburg, the other streets around it were full of flophouses. So Sandburg Village was like a military operation. We had to have the sufficient size and numbers to go in there and push the enemy back. Coldly. Like D-Day.
john cordwell, chief architect of Carl Sandburg Village

the apartments were new & beautiful & appeared out of nowhere. my moms parents worried she moved so close to Cabrini, so close, to so many Black people. she left junior college, got a job selling downtown at a department store. she moved in with her friend Helain. flocks of young white people came to the new Sandburg Village, built as a buffer between the wealthy center, a growing Puerto Rican neighborhood to the north & high-rise projects housing Black lives like a prison to the east. the management so paranoid & adamant in their protection of the downtown hold, they put the national guard on top of the roof during the rebellion after Martin King was murdered. the onslaught they feared, never came.

there was a pool on the roof, an alluring feature. my father gigged there as a lifeguard. it was his third. one at a bar, one at a school. he lived close with his buddy Gary, in a coach house at 1338 North LaSalle. he moved from Edgewater south to be near the gigs & a growing scene of college grads beginning to nightlife on Division Street. what were these young whites called then: intruders, pioneers, pawns. in struts my mother, one afternoon, my father on duty. he asked to see her key, her membership for admission. she was not having it that day or any in her life & promptly gave him the finger, the middle, with the quickness. she complained in tones unnecessary for a saturday at 2. my father listened, nodded, waited til she finished, then, unmoved, still asked to see her key. she chucked them at the table. the keys hopped into his hand like a shortstop. my pops was impressed, surprised by the flex. she walked away before he could say anything. he saw her pass, in all her glory, and his weak, lone response was: *damn.*

after cooling off in the chlorine she apologized by flirting. invited him & Gary for dinner that night. they cooked & ate & talked about people they might have in common, the convention, the riots, all the change the city/country was mired in. my father worked at a bar called the Store, not far on Clark Street. Helain & my moms went. he poured drinks. she watusied. they caught each other's eye & moms mouthed the words *i love you.* she was wild like that, reckless cause she had nothing. my father looked behind, around, shocked, put a finger to his chest, mouthed a question back: *me*. she nodded & kept dancing.

she stayed on a stool, an elbow, & waited for him. they went back to her place, in the Sandburg Village & they each swear all they did was talk night, into the new day, witnessing the morning in her new apartment, getting to know one another in the new city/country, changing by fist & fire.

Wall of Respect
August 27, 1967

white people can't stand / the wall...Black beauty hurts them—
Haki Madhubuti, *The Wall*

picasso ain't got shit on us[8]

so said the nine who portrait-ed:
Malcolm & Muhammad,
Nina & Bird, Marcus & Amiri
at 43rd & Langley.

a few weeks after
the bird/woman sculpture
revealed politicians don't know
much bout anything, 'specially art.
on the side of a tavern
next to Johnny's tv & radio repair
a store that fixes the image, the wall
a shrine to Black creativity.

a 24-hour gallery where little girls
could see women who looked
like their mother. the people
came, *a Black stampede.*[9] a gathering
spot, an outdoor museum, no entrance
fee, free. a Black festival of chromatics
body & hue.   from here
street art & public mural
movements. walls & spray cans
will sprout, a people's art.
the city, a canvas.

AfriCOBRA
1968

African Commune of Bad Relevant Artists.
bad the way Run-DMC defines it. a crew
trying to transcend the *i* for *WE*, Muhammad Ali.
relevant like how most art ain't cuz institutions
beholden to the loaned collections of the rich
& they don't want a painting holding a knife
to their neck.

Jeff Donaldson, Wadsworth Jarrell, Gerald Williams,
& Barbara Jones-Hogu made Kool-Aid colors for superReal
people. colors the people would be drawn to: the luster
of a just-washed head, the glint of sunglasses, grandparents'
shea-butter sheen, Afro puffs & a girl in a yellow overcoat.

after them: Kerry James Marshall, SLANG
Krista Franklin, Hebru Brantley, Amanda Williams,
art that hasn't been made, prints created
so an 8-year-old in Woodlawn or L-Town
may wake every morning & see themselves.

The Assassination of Chairman Fred Hampton

December 4, 1969

the Panthers came home to the West Side
near Chicago Stadium where the bulls play
& no memorial sits. a statue for mike
but nothing for Mark Clark & Chairman Fred.

what shook hoover: Black children eating
breakfast, starting the day with sustenance
& the free conversation between the real rainbow
coalition: Young Lords & Young Patriots,
the non-aggression pact the Panthers negotiated
an alliance of street organizations that loved
the second amendment a lot & Black people
the most.

secobarbital, a sedative, was slipped in his drink
by an informant. Fred to sleep forever in the blood bed
next to Akua, 8 months blooming. at 4:45am cpd & fbi
bust thru the door, knew exactly where the Chairman
was cuz the blueprint, cointelpro. 2 shots point blank
into the mind of a genius. Fred of Maywood, 21 years
old, executed by the state for being with the proletariat
against the pigs. the last words on his lips:

i am a revolutionary

Don L. Lee Becomes Haki Madhubuti

1972

lee was not a revolutionary name:
an ill fit after the army he served
& left, after his mother's decline & death,
after reading Richard Wright & seeing his
body in Black   for the first time.

Haki was given by a committee of ancestors.
a reclamation & renaming. they allowed him
to reintroduce himself: Haki means justice.
Madhubuti is four syllables, means precise.
means dependable. what other poet/writer
teacher been more dependable in the struggle
for justice.

Haki Madhubuti means long haul & fire, means
the work for real, means storefronts will blossom
to Black institutions, means build with Black stones
means anybody down to build, means by any, reinvention
of the world, the word to burn. lee an effigy to the white
wor(l)d left behind   smoldering & ashy.

Haki Madhubuti means the Black future ahead.

The Chicago 21 Plan
September 1973

oak and chandelier. opaque light
filtering thru the day's death. an ash
tray near each fat white hand.
the original canopy of cigar smoke.
what is meant by back room dealing.

a plan to centralize in the loop.
to build a mote, a fortress. a gold
coast. gold mine. mine. take dead
tracks & build condos. river norths.
south loops to stave off white flight.
to usher white folk into condos.
into printers row. choke Cabrini
of its green.

pay to play. pay to stay. everyone was in
on the act. the universities & big businesses.
hold the center. transform blues to white
collar. daley to daley. Black to white. flight
from the past. erasure by another name:
gentrification's birth certificate.

Leaving Aldine
1978

my pops wanted to make his own
name. build a restaurant with his on it.
my brother was not yet. i was & remember
the movers. the men who worked & drove
a truck as i would. there was not a lot left
in the apartment. soon there would not be
my pops in the house.
                          but before
at the window, i was
playing with the blinds. spider
man on the television not yet
repossessed. the bead chain
my web. my earliest memory
the apartment, the city. a hope
something would make me   stick

Ode to Steppin

1978

when you could only buy 78s
& the jitterbug slowed to smooth.
when the lindy hop landed
in a little bit of bread & the hawk
adorned the body in long coats
& fox furs. when gents were majestic
& ladies mirrored the men, one foot
at a time, but did it backwards
meaning they went harder
but you couldn't tell cuz the glide
& off time cool was no sweat at all.
when Jeffree Perry should've been
a star & Black Mary was Chicago's Queen,
stepper sets filled Bronzeville ballrooms
& basements & weekend banquet halls.
when people's parents still married
or at least together cuz of the kids.
when you could raise a family in the city
E&J away a weekend with a woman
in one hand & a handkerchief in the other.
when you were a gouster or ivy league.
when high or low end wasn't a death sentence.
when the middle class was an aspiration
the city/country seemed to believe
& folks could take some time to get there
at least til Monday or at least til Sunday
morning when the lights would come on
like the sun at the lake no one could afford
to live near. when the weekend was over
but *love's gonna last* like the stubborn couple
at the end of the night, when the DJ's gone
quiet & the chairs overturn on tables
& the turntables tumbleweed
but the 4/4 still ghost-steps
in their bodies at the end of the dance
floor, quiet as they float above
portable wood tiles or taut linoleum
as one. when one night is all
anyone ever needs.

Disco Demolition

July 12, 1979

White males . . . see disco as the product of homosexuals, blacks, and Latins, and therefore they're the most likely to respond to appeals to wipe out such threats to their security.
Dave Marsh, *Rolling Stone*

steve dahl donned a helmet
a military uniform, drove the diamond
in an army jeep. dahl was a white
middle brow disc jock. his listeners
white men in the middle of america.
factories were packing up. the world
promised began to look other/wise.

dahl & white sox management
made a promo night to attract
a dwindling fan base
in a subpar season.
it was 98 cents to get in
if fans brought a record
to be blown up in center field.

Disco was dance
for the generation after Vietnam.
sped up Soul dreamt in Gay
clubs, Black & Latino & more.
& the whites came
& the whites came.

tonight they came, aroused
with beer & records to burn.
a vinyl bonfire. Black records
aflame.

comiskey park
in bridgeport, home of the dick
daleys. they fell in love with their mother's
corned beef & cabbage & an architectural
appreciation for viaducts.

white men hopped turnstiles, ticket lines.
more bodies crammed in comiskey
than there'd ever been. Chicago was playing
Detroit. cities dwindling like the white majority.

dahl set the fire. a ringmaster,
a comic imp, a cowardly warlord.
a small pop & boom! fans
stormed the field, littered
the grass with bottles & concession debris.
records sliced the air like weapons.
long hairs in lee jeans & cut-off
t-shirts slid into second. they stole home
again. a crater burned into center
field. a white mob on the diamond.
the game postponed, forfeit, rigged
from the beginning. Harry Caray couldn't
control the crowd or get them back
in their seats. the police were called:
uncles & fathers came to chase
their sons. the force restrained.
no one was shot or beat to death.
there were scoldings, few arrests.
steve dahl walked free.

                    Chicago
                    would grind disco in a steel mill
                    run it thru electric sockets til it bumped
                    grimy. til it was House & jacked
                    the body. til the technology
                    displaced white disc jocks.
                    made them obsolete, old machines
                    dancing in their graves.

mayor byrne Moves Into & Out of Cabrini Green

Easter Sunday, April 19, 1981

the first night
the mayor & her husband
watched the academy awards,
april fools in a two-bedroom
apartment furnished
by montgomery ward
in the most infamous
project on the planet
protected by 2 bodyguards
6 squad cars. her publicist
said she'd return to her gold
coast apartment a few blocks
east for a change
of clothes or perhaps a week
end, tho residents saw her sneak
in every morning & out each night
                 for three weeks   she lasted.

& such is whiteness

the ability to de-robe
a life/style & return to privilege
awash in skin, adorned in birth
rite. a retreat, a return
back across heavily patrolled
borders of wealth
& white / working & not   white.

on easter the mayor's blonde
ambition presides over an egg
hunt, the residents picket,
chant: *we need jobs, not eggs*
jane byrne is the ku klux klan

the mayor as invader
conquistador, missionary:
idyllic words backed by force.

on the day Jesus returns
the mayor flees.

54

Ron Hardy Plays the Record Backwards
The Music Box. 1982–1987

I can imagine him praying before he put on his turntables.
Adonis, Chicago acid house pioneer

Robert Williams gave him the run of the place.
a playground of speakers. an open studio to mad
scientist. shirt open, he'd dr. frankenstein sound.
stitch Black soul to new wave. one afternoon
high as shit, he must've flipped. turned the needle
upside down, spun the tone arm over, propped the wax
on a cylinder to keep it spinning, pushed the platter
to earth & played it backwards. on beat. his mind
forever changed. on heroin, the music slowed to a nod.
he sped it up. dancers jacked new velocities. sent
a generation to their parents' record collections
to rescue history. to dig & cut it up. resuscitate it
for the people to feel in a way that could move them
to (a)movement. break & pose & vogue before madonna
stole. before it was called that. from Chatham, a whole
city seeking sanctuary on his dance floor to get loose
& live & high, to find themselves aligned.
a fix, of chaos, in order to get free.

The Assassination of Rudy Lozano

June 8, 1983

a man driven by a search for unity among people
Harold Washington on Rudy Lozano

he was kicked out of high school
looking for Latino history. his curiosity
built Juarez, rivers at Cermak & Ashland.
Pilsen, his home. Harold, his homie
he helped elect thru organizing
the neighborhood & Del Rey tortilla
workers. mustache like a push broom.
a texas Chicano, Chicago son
whose sister & sons fight sin
fronteras. the city
so shook, it armed itself.
sent a 17-year-old
into the summer night
into the Lozano kitchen
with a hammer trembling
before the scariest architectural
idea: a bridge built between
Black & Brown workers, a class
alliance, a border crossing.

Marc Smith Invents the Poetry Slam
1984

the city's a racket
so loud you can't hear yourself shit.
space for quiet some yuppie luxury.

Marc built homes with his hands.
moved metal, lunch pail, hot thermos
to a saloon. in the evening stories came.

the apple fell on his head
after work at 1758 North Honore
the Get Me High Lounge:
red lamps, music ledgers
lining the john, smoke
& flannel everywhere:

america loves sport
but needs story.

he handed scorecards to the regulars.
Tony Fitzpatrick, the referee.
Patricia Smith, the city's empress.

Marc stood on top of a table
in his father's coat & pulled a poem
from night. part Sandburg
part Saul Alinsky, for a few seconds
the din sunk to the floor. even the drunks
listened, remembered their own
mother, their bum day, an outrage.

the poem no longer untouched
in a museum. it paraded the streets
on the shoulders of giants & pigeons.
it sat in a church hat on the bus
& wound its way into the throats
of every man, woman & non-binary
being.

as he spoke the last word,
a locomotive rumbling
into the station, gasping
screeching, letting the steam
out, he extended his hand
& ear to hear all the words:
& he pulled the next one up
& the next one
& the next

Collateral Damage
1985

coke was cheap & stacked
on tables, hidden in cute purses
in glass vials. around at lunch time
at the merchandise mart
where moms moved lines
for big stores carrying the latest fashion.

         i don't think she's
who the CIA envisioned as clientele.

she's young & single & struggling
to make rent. she'd hit Faces,
the disco on rush street & come home high
& not make rent. & we'd move again.
the suburbs our diaspora:
the divorce took us from Sanders Road.
there was the ranch house on Walters.
the townhome in Pheasant Creek.
the one near mama.
the one behind the Phillips '76.
the one behind white hen.

         i'm forgetting a few.

white had a hold of my family
too. my home, a chess piece,
a chair holding a parking spot
in the snow, a vacated split
level. an eviction, notice: white
working. we lived in cooked
county.

The Day Harold Died
November 27, 1987

we went to the rock & roll mcdonald's the wednesday before thanks-
giving. moms took a half-day. she was fly & a fashion rep—high on a
mound of white. i was 12 & lived with Harold for four years. he was
somewhere between Malcolm X & Martin King & a Black grandfather
whose feet i wanted to sit at. he was barack before barack; a Chicago
hope, a Chicago King who brought Latins & Blacks together like Frank-
ie Knuckles. the first Black mayor in the city of DuSable.

the rock & roll mcdonald's was filled with sequined capes, shiny 50s bar
stools, elvis/beatles posters in half a hall of fame of white-washed mem-
orabilia. not a Buddy Guy pic in sight, not a Howling Wolf guitar lick on
the jukebox. in the city of Muddy Waters the golden arches were a white
heaven where jump blues turned vanilla shake.

i knew i didn't like white music & was beginning to know the extent
white people lied on history & in the parking lot that day i knew a lunch
out with moms & my brother was a luxury. i knew this was how rich
people must live, ordering, off menus. i knew at any time things could be
taken away; electricity, fathers, mothers in handcuffs.

we ate in the car. moms juggling a fleeting to-do list in her brain. my
brother, a boy monk in the front seat trying to visualize some future
stability. his heart still, a soft fruit, sweet. he carried toys in his pocket,
wanted a transformer for Hanukkah, hoped that what we were, was not
the limit of what we could become.

the car was on cuz the hawk[10] was swooping between buildings on On-
tario & Ohio like a flood & the radio was audible & murmuring, tuned to
WBBM or WGN or maybe even GCI if moms let us have a say that day,
for once in our life. we were mid-bite in the damp & growing cold of no-
vember & the radio whispered, Harold was dead. it was the afternoon &
i didn't think someone could leave with the sun still out, a giant shining
overhead like some Moses, some Tubman, promising a possible land. the
radio said he sipped his coffee, slumped at his table, his heart attacked &
he was gone.

i thought we'd have to move next, like when the landlord says go.
The Mayor was gone & soon too, the people.

Patronage

February 29, 1992

*If I can't help my sons then they can kiss my ass! I make no apologies to anyone. There
are many men in this room whose fathers helped them and they went on to become
fine public servants. If a man can't put his arms around his sons and help them, then
what's the world coming to?*

richard m. daley, January 2, 1977

a city of stupid sons. boys being
boys. stealing their father's new white
chevy blazer & driving an hour & a half
around the U of the lake to their summer home
in michigan to get turnt & let off catholic boy
steam & drink, pull out a shotgun, a baseball bat
& beat an indiana boy's brain to blood clot.

no daley will serve
time. time is for other sons
without birthright. without a firm
that will receive millions in sewage
contracts, shit money filling up
bank accounts or the internet
contract for o'hare or the tur global
investment firm where daley & his boy
sell off Chicago's public goods
to the highest bidder. bitter
men & their dumb sons.

daley's daddy made his son
the state's attorney despite failing
the bar twice & never trying
a case. when evidence of police torture
graced his desk in the early '80s
it was ignored. his ignorance made him
mayor.
      & what
      father wouldn't
want to stand for his son.
make a call or tell a judge
over lunch at the Chicago club

to take it easy, let the family
handle it.
                patronage
is a Chicago word for family
for taking care of one's own
& what father would disagree
or wouldn't want to spare his son
from jail or death, a desire for a life
easier than his own.

Fresh to Death

Summer 1992

In Chicago, police created a whole new crime category, Starter Jacket Murders
Jet Magazine, May 11, 1992

starter jackets were the coldest
second skin. they'd glitter
in the wholesale windows
of Maxwell Street storefronts
like flags or primary-colored
emeralds. shone from Black
poets on Yo! MTV Raps.
Chicago, Hornets, mascots, cities
emblazoned on the chest
like tribal tats, religions, gang
affiliations. clean sport cuffs
& collar. snap buttons & sheen.
the coolest wore them open even
in the crisp air, airing rope gold
& white tees. a coat perfect
for the fall. so much loot, you'd
get slapped just for thinkin
bout askin your mama for one.
oil-slick arms just outta reach
like everything in america.
so cold it seemed reasonable
this could be the ocean of satin
somebody might die over.

Molemen Beat Tapes
1993

were copped from Gramaphone.
cassettes jammed into the factory
issued stereo deck of the hoopty
i rolled around in. a bucket. bass
& drum looped with some string
sample, fixed. a sliver of perfect
adjusted. the scrapes of something
reconstituted. there was so much
space to fill. an invitation to utter.
Iqra- Allah said to the prophet
Muhammad (peace be upon Him).
a to b-side & around again. a circle
a cipher. i'd drive down & back
in my moms dodge for the latest
volumes of sound. i'd stutter
& stop & begin again. lonesome
& on fire. none. no one i knew
rapped. i'd recite alone on Clark Street
free, styling, shaping, my voice
a sapling, hatchling, rapping
my life, emerging in the dark
of an empty car.

there was a time when hip-hop felt like a secret
society of wizards & wordsmiths. magicians
meant to find you or you were meant to find
like rappers i listened to & memorized in history
class talked specifically to me, for me.

& sometimes
you'd see a kid whisper to himself
in the corner of a bus seat & you
asked if he rhymed & traded a poem

a verse like a fur pelt / trapping.
some gold or food. this sustenance.

you didn't have to ride solo anymore.

✳

Jonathan was the first kid i met who rapped. he was Black
from a prep school, wore ski goggles on top his head & listened
to Wu-Tang which meant he was always rhyming about science
& chess. his pops made him read Sun Tzu. his mans was Omega
a fat Puerto Rican who wrote graffiti & smoked bidis.

& they'd have friends
& the back seat would swell
& the word got passed / scooped like a ball
on the playground. you'd juggle however long
your mind could double-dutch. sometimes you'd take
what you were given / lift off like a trampoline
rocket launch. sometimes you'd trip & scrape
your knees. tongue-tied, not quick. words stuck
on loop, like like words, stuck, like that. but break
thru, mind, knife sharp, mind darts
polished & gleaming we'd ride
for the sake of rhyming. take the long way
home or wherever the fuck we were going
cruise down Lake Shore & back, blasting
blazing. polishing these gems.
trying to get our mind right.

Graffiti Blasters: An Erasure (A Buff)
1993[11]

Graffiti   scars   hurt

            Chicago
        blast   trucks
        use baking soda   high
        pressure   remove
        stone   mineral.
a model
        for other cities foreign
        WarsawPragueMilanChina   Arizona
the City's anti-crime   program
                depends
                on removal   we make every effort
                to remove.

The Department works very closely   with Police   will apprehend
vandals
                        deface.

No Chicago   has to tolerate   graffiti.
Please join us   in eliminating   a beautiful city

The Violent Crime Control & Law Enforcement Act

September 13, 1994

made the streets gaunt
ghost like. gave daley
the impetus to cut heads
of gangs with abandon
& no oversight. 100,000
new police. 9.7 billion for
mass incarceration. inmate
education no more
Malcolms or Etheridges.
jail rigid, more separatist.
more private stock
options on how to pile
minors. magicians
making students
vanish, school to prison
pipeline, urban out
fitted, since this bill
clinton passed & rahm
rammed thru congress
making democrats
republican. when the country
tricked the huddled masses
the poor & tired deported
kids kidnapped off the block.
there's a 33 percent chance
each Black man will be
in chains again. 3 strikes
means life. means gone
til november like the jobs.
means the 13th amendment
applies here, means you can't
apply here. jobs obsolete.
delete. means you'll be
deleted. defeated. the city
creates an indentured
servitude, a new service
sector. a new slavery.

The Etymology of Chicago Joe
September 27, 1994

> *Slim was fresh, Joe*
> **Common, "I used to love H.E.R"**

in Chicago, we call men *Joe*

from the hebrew, *Yosef*
Jacob's eleventh son. Jesus's stepdad.
as in Louis, Frazier, DiMaggio.

as in cup of. *Joe Blow*
an average fellow. a generic man.
G.I. with the kung-fu grip
though most *Joes* have trouble
holding a grip. the every man
Algren wrote of, *Joe Felso*
the hustler & hustled.
shoeless & misunderstood
despite hall of fame numbers.

Joe is always looking for work.
Joe is always looking over his shoulder.
Joe gets nervous when someone walks up on him too quick.
Joe gets nervous when cops around.
Joe is illegal.
Joe is an immigrant.
Joe is a regular guy trying to make it
& for that you can get knocked
on the head or worse
in this city. the grind keeps
Joe's nose to the stone
streets paved in potholes.

Joe should have his number retired.
Joe is a retired numbers runner.

too many *Joes* have county-issued numbers.
too many *Joes* numb & unaccounted for.

Joe, a sure thing you can count on
Joe is tired of running.

71

P. BRANTON

Common's Resurrection
October 25, 1994

beloved, know how amped we was:
the first time the culture rooted
in Chicago stories & slang. locales
our own, on the bus to touch home. here
the names of streets we knew, ran. a young
man we'd seen off Cottage, at the jam, heard
on WHPK. he sounded like the city
we loved that will never love us back.
sounded cold, like he had one. on wax
for the whole country to hear. an international
megaphone a dozen years after The Message
loud & clear: the children of Gwendolyn Brooks
are rappers. his pops played ABA ball.
moms, a doctor of education. a Chicago son
speaking what he/we knew: Andre Hatchett,
carfare, jewtown. Stony Isle, DJ Pharris, Leon's
BBQ. high schools we went to, fought with
played against, girls we hollered at. the greatest
extended metaphor hip-hop ever wrote.
monuments for what was/is here. *when*
mad was tall & phat was cold. we loved
Twista who rapped so quick we needed
a translator. DA Smart, Fast Eddie
the super bowl shuffle, a slew of graffiti
writers who went to war with mayor daley
but Common put Chicago at the intersection
of the culture, made Ice Cube an actor. mike
on vinyl, a ring you could hear in the sweetgums
& sycamores. footprints in the sand at lake
shore, a blueprint for the many to come.

The Supreme Court Makes Color Illegal
March 3, 1995

Residents of Chicago will be the losers, for they forfeit the benefits of spray paint.
Justice John Paul Stevens

nothing vivid, nothing out
                    the ordinary, nothing off
grey   scale. out   the lines
of black & white.   (whites only)
               nothing
                    · cops can't read
          think is a gang
every kid
          of color with color
a gang. gang, what
                    is a crew
a community, policed.
even the art, the innovation
gone. brush, color gone.
               a country
of bone & art school.
          everything here illegal:
art, people of color   with color
          nothing with color
nothing that questions
                    that jars the mind
          aware awake.   a wake
only. no spray
paint. bullets ok.
grave markers ok.
targets ok
the store, on backs
of bodies of color with color ok.
          ok   color, the problem.
          color the criminal.
criminalize color, ok. ok.

Erasing the Green
September 27, 1995[12]

tearin down the 'jects creatin plush homes
Common, "Resurrection"

towers torn before 9-11.
gaping wounds. living
rooms gut bare. painted
walls for the city to see
brick tumble into graves, rubble
like barney. the stone age.
headstones for Keisha
& Dantrell Davis. Girl X
marks the spot Candyman
minstreled celluloid screams
in the throats of white america.
an abacus of broken promises.
an aberration too close to gold
coasts. wires wild like snakes. snakes
like banks with redevelopment monies.
HOPE grants. good times filmed here.

& no good times filmed here.
fear of a nation & feeding
frenzies on the carcass. the bare
skeletal dreams of public
housing returning to earth.
dust. ghost. memory. maybe
raise three-bedroom townhomes.
the old grocery store where milk
& lottery tickets sold/bought
sandwiched between
young professionals like wonderbread.
cost an arm & leg leg arm head.
no g-d here, unless the church worship
the dollar.
the irony.
the green.

Ida B. Wells Testifies in the Ghost Town
1995–2011[13] in the rubble of the Ida B. Wells Homes

this is not the white city,
though perhaps it is a city
for whites. these are the Southern
Horrors: abandoned streets, boarded
buildings, empty tumbleweed lots.
you can hear Lake Michigan
in a coke can. this barren land
where children once moved
from these blocks to prison
auctioned.

blocks never been safe.

this a Red Record of displacement.
what happens when culture amnesias.
I sat on a train seventy years before
Montgomery. what'll this land be named:
scrapped plan for poor & Black, will it
be Lynchburg or Prisonton, New Laborville
the white city, again. these homes
had my name on them. now

I stand on rhodes near bridgeport,
astonished. prime land, my body, real
estate for the taking. dismembered
by hands the shade of ghost. my body
disfigured, again, this is what happens
when culture amnesias, when cities cancel
its promise, call it renewal. what happens
to those blue light monitored & standardized
test tracked, those forced into obsolete industrial
training, railroaded into new slave labor, orange
suited & disenfranchised, what do we do
with the forgotten, those left   out
to
hang
like ghosts.

I witness until the world does
until ghost stories are documented
& irrefutable, until America is haunted
by the spirits of those it says never happened.

How to Teach Poetry
in Chicago Public Schools
back to school, 1996

look clean. fresh
kicks, cut, jeans. iron
them shits. cuz even in uniform
the baddest student swagger on a 100
& those the kids you hope to build
with. the ones who got a crate
of albums on heart:
Weezy, Gucci, Waka Flocka
some may even have they own
bars for days. spit
alone in their room,
to their girl, a little
brother. they might
be reluctant to share
especially with a teacher
especially with a whiteboy.

start with a rhyme, something
quick. a half note behind
Westside double time.
their ears piqued, able
to roll with all those syllables.
now read a poem. something
slow, familial, familiar
an offering to Gwendolyn Brooks
& Carl Sandburg sitting on your shoulder.

ask where their favorite rapper is from:
J from Marcy
Ye, the South Side
everybody know Wayne
katrina's soldier boy.
from '97 to '03
have a firm, well-reasoned opinion
on who is better: Pac or Big.
after that Young Money, new language
Kanye couplets on memory.

photocopy Willie Perdomo's *Where I'm From*
the wrong way. do this to mess with them
to throw a monkey wrench into normal.
none of us are from Spanish Harlem.
but Englewood know bout police.
every block in the hundreds
got old men who talk shit
guns that fire cracker
grandmothers who stir
big pots. the whole West Side is
littered with nieces telling you
to look past bluebox street lights
cuz regardless of where you from
you from there, you know there
& have never been asked
to expert.

so speak on it.
talk about it.
all you gotta do
is sit that ass down
& write.

Lenard Clark Pedals for Air

March 21, 1997

on the first day of spring
weather might warm
long enough for kids to come outside
again, a miracle in a city where winter
can linger til may.

basketballs & bicycles in need of air
after sitting six months without
bounce & pedal.

in Bronzeville, home of the Black
renaissance, the South Side Community
Art Center, where Ms. Brooks & Margaret Burroughs
meet for tea, Black people have to pay 25 cents for air.

in Bridgeport, home of irish, polish & italian immigrants,
Chicago's mafia & the mayors daley, white folks
get all the air they wish for nothin.

from the windows of the Stateway Gardens
looking west across 12 lanes of the dan ryan express way
where eminent domain is another name for land grab
& colonization, Bridgeport is visible from Bronzeville.

& Lenard Clark didn't want to pay for what should be free
so he pedaled over the expressway & under the bridge & viaduct
into a neighborhood where white boys have been bragging
about keeping Blacks out since 1919.

& Frank Caruso Jr., the son of a guy
in the Chicago mob & two of his classmates
at De La Salle—the all-boys catholic school
of irish mayors & the italian outfit
(& if you think this is the first & last
time the two worked together i got
ocean front property in Cicero
i'd like to sell ya)—these older boys

saw Lenard peddling across borders
& chased the 13-year-old into an alley
& kicked his head into a coma.

this is how Black boys are bar-mitzvahed
in Chicago/america, by boot & brick, his boy
hood/body left deflated   in the alley
so far away   from home.

Baby Come On: An Ode to Footwork
1997

this is tap gone gangster.
in Wolof the Senegalese say dzugu:
to live wickedly. Juke is wicked music
unsanctioned house. a hundred & sixty beats
per minute.
                                    here
folk move. turn the foot
Road Runner & Michael Jackson.
uprock on amphetamine. dance
in the war zone. in the war on drugs
Jack your body became run for your life
in place. on house arrest. take this space
small & make the most of it. glide
then magic, majestic, jack-knife leg
polyrhythm. pirouette stomp.
marionette legs on hot coals
on hot blocks. running man
in a circle or line / up. opposite
of prison. a battle no one gets hurt
most of the time. tip-toe kung-fu   kick
then drag the foot in molasses.
it's all that. all those hidden   Black
magic diasporic movements that might   kill whitefolk:
The Jig & Cakewalk   Pigeon Wing & Ring Dance
       & Capoeira in praise of Shango or DJ Rashad or
              R.P. Boo   or some other deity
       that don't look like a private dick or dick daley.

the foot is furious. the foot is working /   the foot is kicking   that ass
Black on Black time & space travel   sound   barrier   /
       broke
not confined to the speed   /   of the body.
       over   lo-fi low-budget bass   K-town favela funk   /.
       fuck
frenzy. fake out.   ghetto house. James Brown   jumping   bullets.
a ballet of the hustle. no money   no problem.
in the south they spoke Gullah   /   a creole

called it joog,   juke: something disorderly   / not   normal.
the foot   /   body not supposed to move   /   like
     that
not that rubber   band   /   not that   unshackled

          to gravity
                                            /   not that   free

A Moratorium on the Death Penalty
January 31, 2000

     today is a victory   for the hundreds
who persevered
who pushed the impossible
who fundraised in cafeterias
     in church community rooms
     with paper plates & mac & cheese
     made by mothers of sons facing state execution
who believe in Jesus's proclivity to save.
     it took a few journalists
who trust in long hours & interviews
whose reports bloomed above the muck
     & tabloid like lotus.
     law professors at Northwestern
who had an inclination & a class
     of committed students
who sifted thru thousands of documents
who uncovered truths the city hid
who shed new light. A People's Law Office
who filed & pro-bono-ed & argued on behalf of men
who Chicago tortured into confession before guantánamo
     a dark room, a simulated death & electric shocks
     on the watch & under the eye of states attorney richard m. daley
who never investigated or testified to what he knew
who rahm saved before subpoena.

     today is a victory   for the activists
who spend their lives ensuring the lives of others
     will not be taken by a racist state of injustice,
who are prison abolitionists & radical nuns
who are cultural organizers & writers & socialists
who are sisters & mothers & grandmothers
     of the incarcerated

     today is a monument to the moment
     the Death Row 10
     found each other inside
     a rotting system, men

who traded notes & formed a community
     a minyan, a cipher, a crew of support
who fought & wrote prayers in a bottle
who used the prison library
who read & decoded the legalese
who reached out & organized the outside
     from within
who made collage flyers to pass thru prison bars
who communicated & galvanized a movement
     10 to stir the masses
who will become thousands
who stand in for millions
     this city/country has murdered
     & stolen from their homes in the night
     thru decades of police torture & forced confessions
     the justice system blind to its own   white
               supremacy.

     10 men
who in the bowels of county & state max security
     would tell what happened
whose words will rise thru letter
     & recording & shake the governor's mansion
who today declared a moratorium on death
     (maybe to save his own ass & reputation)
               but

     today is a monument
     that will lead to a ban
     to exonerations
     to reparations
     a path for the city/
     country to follow

Praise the House Party

May 17, 2000[14]

after Krista Franklin & Britteney Kapri

praise parents asleep in front of a television after a double or grinding the night of a third shift. *praise* the train i learned to ride: the red to the blue to a bus in the hopes the address was written down right on the quarter-sheet someone photocopied well before there ever was a kinko's. *praise* the desire to sneak out & listen to teenage DJs mash bits of records together that didn't make sense to the ear, new arrangements that propelled us out the house like an odd sonic bat signal so we could grind & jack the body & its parts. *praise* the body & its parts. *praise* the sweat & funk the body makes. *praise* the basement so hot it made the outfit you spent an hour preparing optional. *praise* new shoelaces & an old toothbrush to resurrect your busted kicks. *praise* jean shorts, the shortest ones. *praise* the wop & roger rabbit. *praise* radio shack & the mess of wires jammed into odd-fitting speakers. *praise* the vocational-high-school-know-how-to-rig bass box sub-woofers. *praise* Black hands manipulating black wax. *praise* the pans & knobs & casio keyboards put to use in ways manufacturers never imagined. *praise* the punch that wasn't spiked. *praise* the punch that was. *praise* counterfeit chemists & quarter-juice shamans. *praise* the folk who came to get you when you needed them to. *praise* the lock pick, the lookout, the abandoned loft, the house of squatters. *praise* the friend that told a friend. *praise* the heat between bodies making winter bearable. *praise* the night that becomes day. *praise* the get down, the packed jam. *praise* your mans, an employee with keys to the storage facility. *praise* the factories that shipped jobs elsewhere & the jobs that did stay. *praise* the empty spaces we filled with some old records & new styles & ourselves. *praise* ourselves for passing time, for keeping time & making time stop & making time irrelevant, for forgetting time other than a curfew, when you knew your moms would wake. *praise* your moms waking up & for getting down, back in bed, before she did.

Día de las Madres
May 13, 2001

after they sang "Las Mañanitas" in church
after King David whispered to his beloved
Dawn. after the children gave recuerdos
to their mothers & the husbands rushed
to 26th Street to get last-minute roses, after
all the tamales & elotes & champurrados
were laid out on the nice tablecloth
eaten one last time this sweet sunup,
fourteen abuelitas y madres walked
into an open field at 31st & Kostner
in La Villita/Little Village, South
Lawndale on the West Side & started
a hunger strike on mothers day.
they sought from the city what the city
promised: a school on par with white ones
in white neighborhoods where white kids
learn. the mothers want the same, want
what's fair, want Chicago/america
to treat their hijos with dignity & equity   too.

the field was so big you could forget you were
in the city. for nineteen days there was no food.
tents & chairs, wooded tables & song. art made
under the prairie sky. poems & music left at the feet
of the fourteen who suffered for the future,
who starved for honor long enough to win
honors classes, long enough for the school
to be named Social Justice. proof goliath's weak
his name daley & vallas & the blueprint
for privatized corporate education could
topple from the empty stomachs
of women in solidarity.

dawn has come.
rise up, my darling
sunlight is here

the mothers have won.

Kanye Says What's on Everybody's Mind

September 2, 2005

yo—i'm going to ad-lib a little bit.
Kanye West to Mike Myers

live from 30rock, the Roc boy
in the building tonight. late
registration just dropped. before
waves & tidals stormed the beach
before levees broke, before
the media wd say Black folk
loot & white folk survive.

hands stuck in luxe khakis.
rugby top & gold cross
across the neck. he went off
the top
        of the (astro)dome
freestyled, visibly shook
at the federal response
to Black death.
        ain't no such thing
as halfway crooks. news
bias, his own implication
lack of action, rambling
as waves crash
                in the mind
trying to translate rage
into language, to latch
onto & float. he rescued
ten syllables, a concise
editor of 16s, un-teleprompted
the words typed in his heart...

& Donda had done her job.
lullabied the legacy in her son's ear.
a Chicago State doctor channeling

her colleagues Gwendolyn Brooks
& Haki Madhubuti. their cultural son
storming live tv to tell the planet
what it can't wash over.

I Wasn't in Grant Park when obama Was Elected
November 4, 2008

i was on the ave, listening to the only democracy
i believe in. the longest-running youth open mic
in america. i was listening to the young
& the working, Black & unemployed
& Queer & radical imaginations dreaming
narrating the city/country they see
& fear. we were in a room of a hundred.
the street-lamps of milwaukee ave, our spot
light & faithful ear.
                              downtown
the pageantry projected to the planet
protected by guns & cpd. a Chicago
transplant invoked the dreams
of the founding fathers, not their captives
nor workers. the crowd screamed
droned the chant *yes we can.*
                              we were on the ave
laughing   cuz we don't believe you,
you need more people or different ones. we were
not taken with a president-elect, a united states
senator who stood for war abroad & in the streets
those here tonight have left to be free of, for a few
& devise strategies on how to build the block back
up, for real, not waiting for a trickle down or excuses
bout how a bill becomes a law. we watched school
house rock motherfucker & stay rocking the school
in the city of house & Big Bill Haywood.
our Black presidents are killed & rounded
into prison every day.

i wasn't in grant park when obama was elected
celebrating how great the country is. i was scheming
on the ave, with the people, cooking up a new one.

Republic Windows Workers Sit In
December 5, 2008

> *I would like to encourage anyone who has been in a situation like us that they fight and they demand their rights. They have nothing to lose.*
> **Armando Robles, organizer of the Republic Windows and Doors workers**

organizing began with whispers
in the break room. a tavern
after punch clock.

when the company comes to close
the workers will not leave. for six
days capitalism got its ass kicked.
the workers united will never be
defeated. they refuse to be refuse.
bossman could care less. they sit
like Buddhas, bodies on the line
in lawn chairs with coolers & hot
aluminum wrapped tamales.

the company thought they slick.
opened a non-unionized shop
in Red Oak, Iowa, under the name
echo. & the poems write themselves:
echoes of the Republic for which it stands.
the workers sit. the workers are the best
poets. five years from now will take over
the whole joint, fire the ceo
rename the company: New Era
build a worker-owned co-op
on this day, capitalism lost.

The Night the Modern Wing Was Bombed

February 22, 2010

a 44-foot mural on a 50-foot wall in 14 minutes
during a blizzard at 3 in the morning. caught
security, cpd, the whole city, yawning
slippin, sleeping. writers plottin, creepin
geared up: night vision, fat caps, krylon
in knapsacks, backpacks, bandanna face masks.
fame seekin, names flying in night, not white
game tweakin. limestone brick wall, spray that
new modern wing, dumb loot, schools closed
art cut, this the place that / nothing new. 18 bucks
on public land impossible for the public view.
outside where the public view, outside
where the public do. the anonymous wrote
Modern Art above the student entrance
free class, public school. Made U Look
clean ass / hand style, this ain't /no other crew.
the news peeped game, internets, blogs too.
the museum in they feelings, don't want discourse
bout what the arts will do or what artists do
or why so few Chicagoans hang in the museum
why only dead white motherfuckers on the wall
so few painters of Color, who painting with color
bang the mausoleum / why it cost so much
why the art sucks / why they keep art
for the few, away from the many
modern art bandits / pulled off
the heist of the century. after the statute
of limitations / come get me / we gon build
a statue without limits, wave a W
flag & burn an L in the entry.

When King Louie First Heard the Word *Chiraq*
Summer 2010

it was so hot
freezers became   furnaces.
               all the cheese
     melted from spicy chips.
     eveybody's hands were red.
the air
     a sleeping bag
of blood.
     shoes dangled on telephone wires
 like missiles
     toes
tigers. pick one
block everybody
know somebody
who not
a body
anymore.
       King Louie
must've been coming out the bag
of a crown royal, purple velour wrapped
round his hand, bands, knots, a split
swisher, sweet about his mane of wool.
eyes a flame, feet dipped in Bronze
nikes like the ville, the fire. this time

a kid might've said it slick.
someone's lil cousin making
a geopolitical assessment,
a vernacular ingenious flip
addressing the amount
of violence & occupying forces
responsible for the bodies
& militarization of the block,
for food deserts & desert eagles,
a critical pronouncement
countering the myth
of intervention & the war

on drugs, some little body
                    dropped
                        this Chiraq
out the mouth
like a screwdriver,
running from forces
better funded & more
insidious & sadistic.

        & King Louie
mighta waited for the block
to clear, for the heat to dissipate
like october, the lights to chill
til dusk, as this shiny gem
laid in the street like someone
            lost a dead
president but didn't know it.
he scooped it in his pocket.
touched its smooth Black earth
like obsidian, this history & death
he held close, anticipating the right
moment to share, to say it like a spell,
a whisper he plucked from air & was keeping
for the fall
to come

An Elegy for Dr. Margaret Burroughs

November 22, 2010

if you did not etch metal into Black ink
if you did not travel to learn with the Mexican muralists
if you & Charlie did not think African history
       important to re/member & re/present in Black light
       Black thought, Black ideas in Black minds
       in Black brains
if you did not build an institution in your house & basement
if you did not have a door don l. lee could open
       cuz he needed someone   to talk to
if you were not here, Black Arts wouldn't have been
       mothered in this city. the wall of respect
       wouldn't have risen & burned
       in the imagination of the South Side
if you were not here, no AfriCOBRA
       no South Side Community Arts Center
       no institutions, no memory & images
       of girls at their birthday or portraits
       of Du Bois & Malcolm & heroes
       whi-te cubes wouldn't hold
if you were not here, no honest portrayal of Beauty
       nothing authentic, no celebration
       of African forms
if you & Ms. Brooks were not
       classmates & sisters:
       no OBAC
       no Carolyn Rodgers
       no Angela Jackson
       no Walter Bradford
if you were not here, no Black language
       no Black poetic, no ritual song
       in this segregated Chicago

the lineage is you
& Ms. Brooks
& Haki
& hip-hop
& ALL
pro-Black centered words

which is to say true
words for once that stay
telling it how it is.
ALL the voices needed
you nurtured

if you were not here,
   ALL those words & images
   ALL those pro-Black celebratory songs
   ALL the poets you mother tongued,
   ALL the painters' hands you poured kool-aid colors in
if you were not here, generations of american artists would not be.
   you rescued us from english class
   you took some off the block, posted on the corner
   you told us to dream & imagine & build
      our legacies on the shoulders of those before
   you made us believe Art is a language people need

you lived among the people
Bronzeville whirling & warping your doorstep
   a mess of family & pigeons
   a house full of gems & germs
you were always doing your job
   getting our minds right
   telling the next generation (& the generation after &
   after that)
   to be about something, this is what you left

& you left so much
& you will always be
& you will always be here
in a purple caftan & headdress
in acid mikes with no socks on
   you stayed fresh like that
& you left Us the desire to be fresh
to make & tell
& re/tell
& re/make
& re/main
& re/member
& re/present

always
          here, you are
the heart   of the story/city
in order to re/member ourselves
we must   speak
your name

A Dedication to the Inaugural Poet

May 16, 2011 *for Ms. Chanel Sosa*

after reading at the mayor's inauguration
the poet is unimpressed. backstage
w/ secret service & bureaucratic aides
she is on the phone texting her boo
who is twenty w/ three kids & three baby
mamas. a light-skinned GD
w/ green eyes. she is eighteen. Black
Dominican y Colombian w/ an accent
everyone loves. she's an alternative
high school senior who got her hair did
on the West Side the day before; streaks
of some electric moon & spiked bangs.
her mother is not here. nor her siblings.
the last time she saw her father, he told her
he would kill her.
                  in the procession line
after the ceremony, the poet waits
to be taken to city hall to stand
with multi-hued children the mayor
photo-ops in front of. vice-president
joe biden grabs her hand, says he really felt her
poem (you can see in the video joe's real).
the new old mayor daley brushes by
without a word. gets stuck in the traffic of dark
suits & backs into the poet as if she's not there.
he's posing with the 9-year-old white girl who played
america the beautiful on violin.

the poet is big & grown & not cute
on stage. she is beautiful tributing the river
she swims: Brooks & Sandburg, invoking
Algren & Etta James, a realist blues, the most
honest utterance this day.

the poet is undaunted in the line of aldermen.
unmoved by the mayor's wife's congratulations.

she knows she was asked here to be a flower arrangement.
she knows some lines have been redacted
      by press secretaries & homeland security.
she knows backstage she was just another Black girl
      the archbishop didn't say hello to.
she knows in an hour she will take the red line
      back to Chatham where there is not a grocery store
      or millennium park, where there has not been a new day
      in any of her eighteen years.

she will take the train all the way south
where politicians' promises don't reach.

at the end of this day
she is still poor & working
even if she's heading to college
her family will be, her community,
the young men she loves, who she calls
shadows, will remain, without
any of what the mayor's children have.

Memoir of the Red X

June 27, 2012[15]

after Hebru Brantley

> *When I see the blood, I will pass over you, and the plague shall not be upon you to destroy you, when I smite the land of Egypt.*
> **Exodus 12:13**

blood on the door.
red slashes in a white box.
a warning what lurks.
a warring. a target.
an invitation to squat.
a pyre to blaze. a death
knell for neighborhoods
south, west. marks the spot
families were, industry was.
illiterate's autograph.
mark of danger. great
migration dream catcher.
promise breaker. temporary
detention center before
land grab. body count.
connotes new orleans
homes, haunted. ghosts
here. Malcolm's memorial.
a red cross inverted
perverted. an emergency
no one scrambles to fix.

Chief Keef's Epiphany at Lollapalooza
August 4, 2012

from stage
he can see
thousands
crowd surf
in a gated
Grant Park.
land stolen
by those
who mosh pit.

his whole camp
faces the Great
Lake: eyes on
the prize
on water, some
have never seen.

heat rises
from the ground
like fire in the brush
in the streets.

thousands of hands,
bodies bounce around
mouth every word

pink mouths
around every word

pink mouths
around every n-word.

more shit
he don't
like

Teachers' Strike in the Chicago Tradition
September 10, 2012

> *The assault on public education started here. It needs to end here.*
> **Karen Lewis, CTU president**

the teachers march in Chicago.
red in the streets again, perpetually.
this is a union town, after all
Most radical of American cities:[16]
Nelson Algren would say

this a fight against a mayor
who sold the unions out
to nafta & the clinton white house.

the teachers' strike
in the Chicago tradition
allied with trade unionists
& Pullman porters. in solidarity
with the Haymarket martyrs
& Republic Windows workers.

the teachers honor those who died
in the 1937 memorial day massacre
when cops shot steelworkers.
they honor those who build & built
the country, who ensured the eight-hour day.

in the name of:
Lucy Parsons
Albert Parsons
& Rudy Lozano

in the name of:
Gene Debs
Mother Jones
Addie Wyatt
Jane Addams &
The Pullman Porters

in the name of Studs Terkel
& his red socks
in solidarity, he rocks from the grave
& would've been on the picket line
today, with the teachers
in the long haul
standing with the many
standing with the teachers
firmly rooted in the Chicago tradition:
on the shoulders of giants
who knocked down goliath
fighting the good fight
for the future of All

During Ramadan the Gates of Heaven Are Open

July 14, 2013[17]

the day after not guilty
a sunday, during Ramadan
a town hall for young people
deliberately marginalized.
they assert themselves at the center
of public discourse. of course
where they belong, have always
been. the wooden stage
painted Black in a second-floor
loft overlooking Milwaukee Avenue
& Division Street.

two Muslim women
take the stage. one
after the other. one
in a headscarf. one
not.
          Ashley
survived the foster-care system
was adopted by a hip-hop mother
in Uptown & kinda looks white
but who knows, really. she converted
to Islam in high school. a super volunteer
at IMAN, the Inner-City Muslim Action Network.
she was unsure what to say
but decided to speak
from the heart. when she heard
the verdict she cried & dry heaved
cuz there was nothing inside to throw up.
she is weeping now, telling a room
of young people, who gathered here
cuz they had nowhere else to go,
during Ramadan the gates of heaven
are open. she is fasting & disciplined
like the work & organizing needs to be.

Farwa is Pakistani
in all-Black everything.

she too did not want to speak
but was moved to do so.
this young woman who weeps
open & often, a chronic lament
      & heartache,
is poised today. mourning
in crisis, righteous
she is
moved to tell the story of Ashura,
a day of fasting & rage
where a community does not say *salaam.*
there is no peace today
it is ok
to rage today
to pray today
for patience.

these two women
american *muezzin*
young & brave
& calling us to *adhan*
to *salat*, to pray
where we gather:

Allahu Akbar!
in the name of Emmett Till
in the name of Trayvon Martin
Allahu Akbar!
in the name of Rekia Boyd
in the name of Oscar Grant
Allahu Akbar!
in the name of Fred Hampton
in the name of the many names we cannot name
Allahu Akbar!
Allahu Akbar!

Ms. Devine Explains the Meaning of Modern Art: A Found Poem

Spring 2014

Veteran Art Institute security guard Cookie Devine in the Christopher Williams exhibition at the Art Institute of Chicago regarding the Bouquet for Jan Ader and Christopher D'Arcangelo.

at first i didn't know what it was. just a room with a picture in it. but today a high school group come in & i'm at the other end & gettin worried like i'ma haveta quiet them cuz you know, they rustlin. but once they come past the wall & see this empty room & the lights is dark, they turn back & see there's a picture of flowers on the wall, just one picture, so it mus mean somethin. the students, well they get to quiet. it jus transforms them like they at a funeral or somethin. they shoulders go slack, heads drop in remorse, they rememberin.

i heard one lady say, one of my co-workers, i can't remember exactly what she say but she say, while we passin on shifts, that the flowers are for friends of his who died real young. well this is my opinion, but in Chicago we know what that is. so when kids come into this room & it's uncluttered like a funeral parlor it's supposed to mean the time & space you need to mourn. the white & little light in here is supposed to mean you can think different bout the person who not here anymore. the flowers in that picture is supposed to mean something beautiful, some kind of memory that's there but'll fade away, like the flowers will.

& the students in that room are dead quiet, like they prayin or somethin. i seen it happen. they might not know the artist's name or whatever but they feel what's going on, cuz they goin thru it theyself. they all lost somebody & in my opinion that's somethin, they can respect.

Two Cities Celebrate Independence Day
July 4-7, 2014[18]

1

midwest weekenders
gather at the lakefront.
blue eyes over navy pier.

the breeze has ease,
distant lite jazz. a cacophony
of calm & citronella.

the sky on fire above
the mighty Michigan
boasts. penthouses,

sailboats stock sun-
burnt faces alight in laughter
& lite beer. a lightness

here. a whiteness.
a luxury to hear blasts
& not flinch or think

someone you love is not.
here is not a land of blood
or body. all remains, remain

well. deposit box inheritance.
the future a right. bright. awash
in light. the holiday is every

day

neighborhoods will bloom tonight.

mini-arsenals stockpiled from Indiana.
smoke & fire in the streets & alleys.
corner boys & working fathers make
the sky burn. the light on the block
warms the faces of little ones, mothers
on stoops finally sitting for a moment
to watch dusk turn the color of candy.

bustelo cans are cannons. roman candles
in county men's hands launch fireballs
into the dark, raging against the stars.

downtown the 1812 overture will whisper
gently over the water. but here quarter sticks
of dynamite bass drum a requiem for the fire
crackers take & for those who won't make it

tonight:

Warren Robison, 16, will be shot 20
times by police with his hands in the air.

tonight

Pedro Rios, 14, will run like a boy
until the cops fire two in his back.

small armies overrun the streets.
free & aimless, makeshift orchestras
of whistles, bottles, bombs. the war
of each day, reenacted every

night.

We Charge Genocide

November 13, 2014

> *...the Chicago Police Department is in violation of Articles 2, 10, 11, 12, 13 and 14 of the Convention of Torture, through the cruel, inhuman, and degrading treatment of youth of color in Chicago.*
> **We Charge Genocide UN Shadow Report**

in front of the world eight
Black, Brown, Queer young folk
rock braids & locs & matching t-shirts
that read: *The Chicago Police Dept. Killed
Dominique Franklin* like they did Fred.
in the hall of the United Nations
for half an hour leaning into each other
heads bent in prayer & power calling to Damo,
their homie, tasered while handcuffed
outside a Walgreens with some candy
or toothpaste in his pocket & who is now
no more. this for those who are no more.
for 30 minutes in silence, hands clasped to fists
raised to heaven like John Carlos & Tommie Smith,
the time Rekia Boyd laid in the street
after an off-duty cop shot her in the head.
again & always there is Black death & today
it receives its proper name, its one true
name. Chicago youth stand on the world
stage to mourn & proclaim. to pronounce
formally, finally, in no uncertain terms:

Atoning for the Neoliberal in All
or rahm emanuel as the Chicken on Kapparot
written on the eve & day of Yom Kippur, September 22–23, 2015

> *Do you call that a fast, a day when the Lord is favorable? No, this is the fast I desire: To*
> *unlock the fetters of wickedness, and untie the cords of the yoke, to let the oppressed go free.*
> **Isaiah 58: 5-6**

you are the first jewish mayor of Chicago
but have not lit one yahrzeit candle
for people murdered by the police.

you vacation in montana with the governor,
bring your family to Chile on a whim
& never worry about crossing borders
or encountering their patrolmen
or the rent upon return.

your grandparents sought refuge here.
escaping those trying to end them.
they came, worked, learned, created
a life that enabled your parents to raise you
in the suburbs: the immigrant face of the american dream.

you dismantle the same system from which your family benefited:
union pay, livable wages, park space safe enough to play outside
arts funding to take ballet, a decent well-rounded public education.

the same ladder your family climbed
you kick the rungs from.

if the schools, housing, health care
trauma centers & corners that cause trauma
are fair across this flat, segregated land—
then eat today. every day there is a harvest
on the carcass of the city for sale. the satiated
carve at a distance, plan, map & redistrict
with careless indifference. how many times
have you been to Kenwood, Woodlawn
North Lawndale. what are the names of the people
you know there. what homes have you sat in.

how can you fast
this week, when food
was refused by grandmothers
& educators & organizers
in your backyard, in the front
lawn of a school Chief Keef attended
in a neighborhood you militarize;
more guns & police your solution
to poverty or an extermination strategy.

how can you fast
when you couldn't stand
in the same room with
those on hunger strike.
in a public forum
you don't listen.
you are the antithetical
Studs Terkel

this is not the city he loved
to listen to, not the city
your grandparents were promised

where is your apology
for sending so many jobs elsewhere
for privileging your children's future
& pillaging others'

what do you know of labor
& no savings account & counting
pennies for a pass, for permission to move
or see a movie or museum in this city
of no access & grand canyons of inequity.

your middle name is Israel
it's come to mean apartheid
in the city, you are mayor
& in Palestine, the city
your family colonized.

there is no safety
          said my G-d
for the wicked[19]

for the divvier of cities
for the divider of nations
for the ignorer of horror
for the builder of walls

atone for the smug assuredness
atone for the maintenance of two cities
        stratified & unrecognizable to the other
atone for the bounty of the north side
        the scarcity of the south
        the want of the west
atone for the erasure of the public
        school, space, housing, parking
atone for the centrism, the move right
        the kowtow to corporations
atone for the inconceivable income disparity
        between those funding your campaign
        & those over whom you reign
atone for the city's change
        its whitewash & removable
        workers who used to make it
        work by working
        in jobs with pensions
        & benefits
atone for the benefits we have
        by merely being white
        on the north side of the city
        country where that is enough
        to make you safe & not think
        about driving a car or going
        for a jog or walk outside
atone for the rite to the city
        that's for some, not for all
        not for real

israel means may G-d prevail
& we pray that's real, for real

                                amen

400 Days

October 20, 2014–November 24, 2015
after Nazim Hikmet

in 400 days
        i've gone thru 3 journals
worked
        on 2 books, a play & a movie
            about house music.
i left a lover
        & found another.
lost 2 teeth
        got 4 stitches, broke
            a finger in a fight
& sat in the barber shop for 24 fades
        mostly from Rob at Chicago's Best
except when i'm traveling & i've learned
not to get a haircut while traveling.

        i've had students graduate
grow hair on their face, had sex
for the 1st time. some are starting
        college, a few have
                been shot:
1 thru the lung
        he lived, made a mix tape.
1 in a parked car
        waiting to see his son
who will now have to wait
            forever.
the city has opened
        hundreds
of new restaurants, private social clubs
        closed public schools
put on a halloween parade
        an irish day parade
        a columbus day parade
        a new year's celebration
            erected condos
        targets
           & never once

apologized.
there have been thousands
                of masterpieces
        artists painted
                on the streets
for the people. but
        the city removed
                cuz art is racialized
                        & the city
        thinks some artists
                        criminal.
i started
        eating chicken again
in the last 400 days, the doctor said
                less sugar.
the city is chicken
                to apologize
        & will never say anything sweet.
the city makes Black
        a target. a video game
a city of zombies, the walking dead.
        for 400 days cpd, the state's attorney
the mayor's office hid evidence
        tape, bullets
        & didn't apologize
        for any of it.
400 days ago
        toddlers were not
yet & now cry thru the night.
        they see a city
of ghosts. walking
        Laquan, the other
way, still shot
        16 times.
no life
        in the eyes
of cops, anita. mayor rahm
looks dead
        into the camera
                & lies
        for 400 days

                    the cubs threatened
        victory
                    but justice
            will have to wait
    til next year

The Night the Cubs Win the World Series

November 2, 2016

my pops chariots a drunken lady
home safely. they pull to the side
of the road in the dark of West Irving
Park & listen to one out, then two, then
weep at the blast of the improbable
come.

i too have tears when talking
to him finally. he is in the melee
of the night trying to celebrate, trying
to hustle the loot for whatever number
mortgage he's on, before the banks pounce
like Kris Bryant on a grounder & throw him out.

we imagine this is for all the fathers
weeping, the mothers' names that chalk
the wall, the grandparents who couldn't
be here. the generations who loved
without hardware, but this is
the arrogance of the north side
incarnate. the double play, double
standard turned over like property.

The Cubs did not win the World Series
tonight. a game in north america maybe
the nation's pastime. but the curse is
not lifted in the shadow of the bloodiest
weekend of the year
                         though the north side
celebrates its constant win. its distance
from the south & west. a delight, a dream
team that's not, but reads so white,
a side so white, they're dumping beer
on each other's heads to metaphor
the excess. what world are we celebrating.

all week long the minstreled indian
smiles from the arm of the Cleveland

hitters as Natives are mauled by dogs
& gas in Cannon Ball, North Dakota
defending their home base & water supply.

the mayor keeps popping up
on camera smiling like a jackass.
the owner upholds the trophy
in the club house & writes checks
to the campaigns of fascists
in the mist of champagne.

the blue flag flying the W
stands for whiteness & blue lives.

i can't celebrate the one side
or one story. not for a single
night or 108 years or 180.

i can't cheer for this
national pastime
of curses fixed
for generations;
redlined, red blooded
american & perennial.

Chicago Has My Heart
March 4, 2017

don't ask me to leave
don't force me to go
when the coasts call
when the rents rise
when the city i know
is unrecognizable.
it's mine, not alone
not to own.

Chicago has my heart
at the lake, on the train
in the first days of spring
that remind us why we live
here, at all, have bodies
can use them outside the cold
restrictions of clothing, the confines
of neighborhood.

Chicago has my heart
the land i'm most confident:
give me an address, i'll get us
there. i know the grid, blocks
got people in these streets
students whose family
run the breakfast spot
on 79th near Haki
who is still here
building temples
to Black lives, monuments
to Mama Gwendolyn

my family is here. my father,
six blocks from me in Albany Park,
the mayor of the city's broke dreams
he holds them in his growing belly
his breaking heart, falling
asleep in front of the television
chatting thru the night in his taxi

the city with money calls an uber,
he drives new residents to wherever
they wish to go. thank G-d
for the hustle, the hustler, my father
the kindest, most incompetent
businessman here. he doesn't
swindle or cheat, he is honest
& fair, what a sucker
this city makes of sweet
men.
       like me
i guess, i just
want justice
& someone
to read poems to
to u

Chicago, my heart
is all the people
who make it
who are making it
barely, in the 77 hoods.
i hate the viaducts
the millionaires
who urban plan them
from the suburbs
they resurrect
downtown

Chicago you have my heart
my whole history, my people
you saved, seeking refuge here
tucked in apartments in Ukrainian
Village & North Lawndale.
you saved them from history
while destroying others'.
my mother left. my brother
moved. my friends gone:
too much rent, debt
you killed some off
you are a ghost mound

i stalk, still, Chicago
you have my heart
split in two
like the city
& stories you tell
but i am one
not two
i am one
second will not do
you can't continue
to break us
in two, in remade
refurbished, renewed
models for the few.

Chicago has my heart
                  but

my head
my hands
my body
with the people
who build
who have a limit
& can break
& tear
it down & stop it
from becoming
what it's becoming

what is it becoming

Chicago has my heart
                  but

the hearts of those
who call this home
who root & champion
the losers & villains
who run this place
who put on for the shitty
pizza & arctic weather

we will turn our backs
on the very land we are
locked in, turn our backs
on the capital wage-slaves
you've made us become.
we will burn your memory
in effigy & house dance
in the afterglow

we rise, Chicago
this body
politic will rise
our fire will burn
again

Notes

1   X names of the Native signees: To-pen-e-bee, his x mark; Sau-ko-noek, his x mark; Che-che-bin-quay, his x mark; Joseph, his x mark; Wah-mix-i-co, his x mark; Ob-wa-qua-unk, his x mark; N-saw-way-quet, his x mark; Puk-quech-a-min-nee, his x mark; Nah-che-wine, his x mark; Ke-wase, his x mark; Wah-bou-seh, his x mark; Mang-e-sett, his x mark; Caw-we-saut, his x mark; Ah-be-te-ke-zhic, his x mark; Pat-e-go-shuc, his x mark; E-to-wow-cote, his x mark; Shim-e-nah, his x mark; O-chee-pwaise, his x mark; Ce-nah-ge-win, his x mark; Shaw-waw-nas-see, his x mark; Shab-eh-nay, his x mark; Mac-a-ta-o-shic, his x mark; Squah-ke-zic, his x mark; Mah-che-o-tah-way, his x mark; Cha-ke-te-ah, his x mark; Me-am-ese, his x mark, Shay-tee, his x mark; Kee-new, his x mark; Ne-bay-noc-scum, his x mark; Naw-bay-caw, his x mark; O'Kee-mase, his x mark; Saw-o-tup, his x mark; Me-tai-way, his x mark; Na-ma-ta-way-shuc, his x mark; Shaw-waw-nuk-wuk, his x mark; Nah-che-wah, his x mark; Sho-bon-nier, his x mark; Me-nuk-quet, his x mark; Chis-in-ke-bah, his x mark; Mix-e-maung, his x mark; Nah-bwait, his x mark; Sen-e-bau-um, his x mark; Puk-won, his x mark; Wa-be-no-say, his x mark; Mon-tou-ish, his x mark; No-nee, his x mark; Mas-quat, his x mark; Sho-min, his x mark; Ah-take, his x mark; He-me-nah-wah, his x mark; Che-pec-co-quah, his x mark; Mis-quab-o-no-quah, his x mark; Wah-be-Kai, his x mark; Ma-ca-ta-ke-shic, his x mark; Sho-min, his x mark; She-mah-gah, his x mark; O'ke-mah-wah-ba-see, his x mark; Na-mash, his x mark; Shab-y-a-tuk, his x mark; Ah-cah-o-mah, his x mark; Quah-quah, tah, his x mark; Ah-sag-a-mish-cum, his x mark; Pa-mob-a-mee, his x mark; Nay-o-say, his x mark; Ce-tah-quah, his x mark; Ce-ku-tay, his x mark; Sauk-ee, his x mark; Ah-quee-wee, his x mark; Ta-cau-ko, his x mark; Me-shim-e-nah, his x mark; Wah-sus-kuk, his x mark; Pe-nay-o-cat, his x mark; Paymaw-suc, his x mark; Pe-she-ka, his x mark; Shaw-we-mon-e-tay, his x mark; Ah-be-nab, his x mark; Sau-sau-quas-see, his x mark.

2   Opening of the Union Stockyard.

3   The last writings of Albert Parsons, published in the *Alarm*, November 5, 1887, a week before his execution.

4   Italics are phrases from Debs's speech upon his release from prison November 23, 1895, quoted in the *Chicago Chronicle* & Karl Marx's *Capital*.

5   A section of German criminal code that made homosexuality a crime from 1871 to 1994.

6   Founder of the political Latino street organization the Young Lords.

7   *Division Street: America* is published.

8   A line from Haki Madhubuti's poem "The Wall."

9   A line from Gwendolyn Brooks's poem "The Wall."

10 "The Hawk" refers to Chicago's cold wind. Used in the *Chicago Defender*, October 20, 1936, and famously in Lou Rawls's 1967 *Dead End Street*.

11 Language removed from the cityofchicago.org website.

12 The demolition of Cabrini Green housing begins.
13 Housing and Urban Development begins and ends demolition of the Ida B. Wells Homes in Bronzeville.
14 City Council passes a rave ordinance, a stricter enforcement of the juice-bar ordinance of April 1, 1987.
15 City Council passes an ordinance marking "dangerous buildings" with red Xs in order to warn first responders about "structural conditions" in "buildings that could create danger for crews responding to fires. These conditions include weak truss or other roofing systems, missing mortar, rotted or damaged timbers."
16 Big Bill Haywood was a socialist and one of the founders of the Industrial Workers of the World, started in Chicago in 1904.
17 The day after a Florida jury finds the murderer of Trayvon Martin not guilty.
18 Eight-two people were shot this weekend. Fourteen of them died.
19 Isaiah 57:21.

Illustration Credits

Acknowledgments

teamwork makes the dream work. i lean heavy on my community, my family forged in blood & fire. Moms, the fighter. Pops, the storyteller. Aunt Joyce, who has transitioned, my Chicago guide to the art hustle. she loved the city, its artists, put on for them & carved spaces for them to grind & shine. my Uncle Steve, the writer & historian, who loves NYC like i do this burg, a civic pride like Jane Jacobs. my brother Eric, the mensch & disciplined educator & father. my sister Elyse, the who manages to put up with my family with grace & light. Addison & Colin, niece & nephew, who are so different & hilarious & lovely & free. Cheryl & Sasha, y'all a badass, amazing duo.

Young Chicago Authors (YCA) is a home & house i built with the many who are there and who have left and who return. Rebecca Hunter, it would be impossible without your vision & dedication to the growth & integrity of this work. To the staff & team at YCA i am indebted to your belief in making the city anew, again, a more better & fresher space for all.

Louder Than A Bomb (LTAB) is a movement. And at this point there have been tens of thousands and more who have participated and made it so. If you care & believe young people, young artists can shape and shift and sing the world as it is & as it will be, this is a space for you to dream, too. This fountain of youth, of freshness & could-give-a-fuck-lessness & care the most, i rock with y'all too tough: the poets & coaches & teachers & volunteers & thousand partners & festival staff it takes to pull off the impossible, salutes.

a generous partner in this work makes this book, *A People's History of Chicago*, possible, The Lannan Foundation and the residency i was able to take in Marfa, texas, where this book really came together. I had a month of isolation, to think & read & write & edit & invest in this project. It was the first time in my life someone said this space is for you to make, that's it, no song & dance, no also teach fifty classes, just create, what a privilege & essential gift & honor.

in texas, i was writing essentially two books & Nate Marshall said to just focus on one. He is the editor, homie & partner in BreakBeats & LTAB/YCA scheming. The student has become the teacher & i am eternally grateful to learn from such an incredible poet & man.

Fatimah Ashgar put eyes on the script & clipped & made essential edits & suggestions & made it more & better. She is an artist with so many talents, who's also an incredible cheerleader, an encourager & champion in your corner.

Jamila Woods is Bonnie. My ride-or-die aesthetic thought partner. There is more music cuz of her syntactical suggestions & presence on the planet.

i wouldn't be alive if not for the brotherhood i share with Idris Goodwin, Hip-Hop's August Wilson. We shit-talked & dreamed a way to change the whole canon.

there are countless other comrades & brothers & sisters in this work. Adam Mansbach, Angel Nafis are two dumb talented & dumb people i love the most.

the folks at Haymarket Books are squad. Anthony Arnove & Julie Fain trust me to create & to have such high-quality brilliant people say yes to your work, your inner turned out, is a blessing. Jim Plank is as down as they come. Sarah Grey is nice af with the editorial eye. Thank you Nisha & Rachel & Caroline & the whole team who make this book & all these words possible.

the artists who blessed these poems with beautiful tributes & portraits i'm forever down for. Hebru Brantley is the homie & GOAT. His downness astounding. His team, Max Sansing, Troy Scat & Bianca Pastel are stupid talents whose work I love & look forward to seeing more & more of. Paul Branton is a true school head whose brush & pen tribute the city of hustlers. Runsy is a former student, whose style & talent have no ceilings.

my mentors are my guides: Bill Ayers & Bernardine Dorn, Rick Kogan, Haki Madhubuti. many informally, but these Chicago institutions have paved a way for me to walk in the world: gatherers of story & song & with a sense of fairness & justice that is unbreakable.

there is a crew around me that make *A People's History of Chicago* real. Brett Neiman has designed every one of my covers & is a renaissance man of the people. Mickayla Johnson, Tammy Job & Nick Ward are out here keeping me grinding & on time. Tara Mahadevan is spreading the word like bo$$ & is high-key the creative director of the whole project. It is a pleasure & honor to work with Ryan at Biz3. & there are many more i am sure i am forgetting & also they many to come. The plan to make this book utilitarian, a spoon or shank or lifeboat. I plan on doing at least 180 readings in 365 days & workshops surrounding the book to have many folk i interact with add their voices & stories to the narrative of this great & troubled city.

so i thank you, the reader, in advance, for holding it down & pushing us forward.

Also Available from Haymarket Books

Before the Next Bomb Drops: Rising Up from Brooklyn to Palestine
Remi Kenazi

L-Vis Lives: Racemusic Poems
Kevin Coval

Long Shot: The Triumphs and Struggles of an NBA Freedon Fighter
Craig Hodges with Rory Fanning, foreword by Dave Zirin

Lucy Parsons: An American Revolutionary
Carolyn Ashbaugh

Mayor 1%: Rahm Emanuel and the Rise of Chicago's 99%
Kari Lydersen

People Wasn't Made to Burn:
A True Story of Housing, Race, and Murder in Chicago
Joe Allen

Schtick: These Are the Poems, People
Kevin Coval

Whiskey of Our Discontent:
Gwendolyn Brooks as Conscience and Change Agent
Edited by Quraysh Ali Lansana and Georgia A. Popoff,
introduction by Sonia Sanchez

About Haymarket Books

Haymarket Books is a nonprofit, progressive book distributor and publisher, a project of the Center for Economic Research and Social Change. We believe that activists need to take ideas, history, and politics into the many struggles for social justice today. Learning the lessons of past victories, as well as defeats, can arm a new generation of fighters for a better world. As Karl Marx said, "The philosophers have merely interpreted the world; the point, however, is to change it."

We take inspiration and courage from our namesakes, the Haymarket Martyrs, who gave their lives fighting for a better world. Their 1886 struggle for the eight-hour day, which gave us May Day, the international workers' holiday, reminds workers around the world that ordinary people can organize and struggle for their own liberation. These struggles continue today across the globe—struggles against oppression, exploitation, hunger, and poverty.

It was August Spies, one of the Martyrs targeted for being an immigrant and an anarchist, who predicted the battles being fought to this day. "If you think that by hanging us you can stamp out the labor movement," Spies told the judge, "then hang us. Here you will tread upon a spark, but here, and there, and behind you, and in front of you, and everywhere, the flames will blaze up. It is a subterranean fire. You cannot put it out. The ground is on fire upon which you stand."

We could not succeed in our publishing efforts without the generous financial support of our readers. Many people contribute to our project through the Haymarket Sustainers program, where donors receive free books in return for their monetary support. If you would like to be a part of this program, please contact us at info@haymarketbooks.org.

Shop our full catalog online at www.haymarketbooks.org.

About the BreakBeat Poets Series

The BreakBeat Poets series, curated by Kevin Coval and Nate Marshall, is committed to work that brings the aesthetic of hip-hop practice to the page. These books are a cipher for the fresh, with an eye always to the next. We strive to center and showcase some of the most exciting voices in literature, art, and culture.

BreakBeat Poets Series titles include:

The BreakBeat Poets: New American Poetry in the Age of Hip-Hop, edited by Kevin Coval, Quraysh Ali Lansana, and Nate Marshall

This is Modern Art: A Play, Idris Goodwin and Kevin Coval

My Mother Was a Freedom Fighter, Aja Monet

Electric Arches, Eve Ewing (forthcoming)

Black Girl Magic, edited by Mahogany Browne, Jamila Woods, and Idrissa Simmonds (forthcoming)